CONFIGURA　　　　　　　　　　**T**

DR. GARY L. VINCENT, PH.D.

CONFIGURATION MANAGEMENT

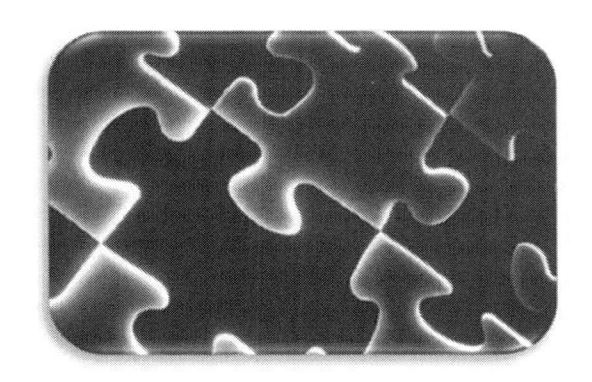

Dr. Gary L. Vincent, Ph.D.

Burning Bulb
PUBLISHING

First Edition

Configuration Management
By **Dr. Gary L. Vincent, Ph.D.**

Burning Bulb
PUBLISHING

Burning Bulb Publishing
P.O. Box 4721
Bridgeport, WV 26330-4721

Orders@BurningBulbPublishing.com
www.BurningBulbPublishing.com

Copyright © 2009 Gary L. Vincent. All rights reserved. No part of this book may be reproduced or transmitted in any form or by any means, electronic or mechanical, including photocopying or recording, or by any information storage and retrieval system without written permission from the author, except for the inclusion of brief quotations in a review and/or parts that were taken from Wikipedia, whose copyright falls under the terms of GNU Free Documentation License.

The Burning Bulb Publishing logo is a trademark of Burning Bulb Publishing.

Edition ISBN

    Softcover 978-1-44869-812-7

First edition.
Printed in the United States of America.

Library of Congress Control Number: 2009908903

Contents

PREFACE 9

CHAPTER 1 WHAT IS CONFIGURATION MANAGEMENT? 11

   The Need for CM 14

   History of CM 17

      Perceptions of Configuration Management 19

      Rising Popularity of CM 21

   CM Standards 24

   Types of CM 25

CHAPTER 2 CM Lifecycle Management 27

   Management and Planning 27

   Configuration Identification 29

   Establishing Configuration Baselines 30

   Configuration Control 31

   Configuration Status Accounting 32

   Configuration and Verification Audit 33

CHAPTER 3 Software Configuration Management 37

CHAPTER 4 Hardware Configuration Management 41

   The CMDB 42

CHAPTER 5 Enterprise Configuration Management 45

   Responsibilities 45

   Preconditions 46

   Tasks 47

   Environments 47

   Work Products 48

Phases 49
    Business Strategy Phase 50
    Business Optimization Phase.....................................53
    Initiation Phase 54
    Construction Phase...57
    Initial Production Phase..59
    Full-Scale Production Phase 60
    Delivery Phase 60
    Usage Phase..61
    Retirement Phase 62
Enterprise Configuration Management Guidelines..........63
CHAPTER 6 Establishing a CM Program 65
    The CM Program...65
    The CM Plan..66
    CM Best Practices 74
    Typical CM Organization Structure..............................76
    Program Phasing and Milestones................................76
CHAPTER 7 CMMI 77
    Capability Maturity Model Integration 77
    Overview...78
    History 80
    CMMI topics 81
        CMMI representation 81
        CMMI Model Framework 81
        CMMI models 84

Appraisal 85

Achieving CMMI compliance 87

Applications.. 88

CHAPTER 8 ISO 9000 93

ISO 9000 series of standards... 94

Summary of ISO 9001:2008 95

Certification... 97

Auditing 99

Industry-specific interpretations 99

Advantages.. 101

Disadvantages 102

CHAPTER 9 PRINCE2 103

History 103

Description of the PRINCE2 method 105

Advantages.. 105

Pitfalls.. 106

Overview of the method 107

Starting up a project 108

Planning... 108

Initiating a project 109

Directing a project... 110

Controlling a stage 111

Managing product delivery 112

Managing stage boundaries 112

Closing a project.. 113

CHAPTER 10 ITIL 115
    ITIL Overview 115
    History 115
    Overview of the ITIL v3 library 118
        1. Service Strategy 118
        2. Service Design 119
        3. Service Transition 120
        4. Service Operation 121
        5. Continual Service Improvement (CSI) 122
    Criticisms of ITIL 123
    ITIL Alternatives 124
APPENDIX A Acronyms 129
APPENDIX B Glossary 139
ABOUT THE AUTHOR 163

PREFACE

Configuration Management is a vast subject that is constantly evolving and improving. It is highly technical in nature with a large amount of content from a wide variety of sources.

Many do not implement CM the same way, thus an endeavor into this field may seem overwhelming or confusing at first glance. It is the intent of this book to take existing data from these multiple sources and aggregate (combine) it into an easy-to-use reference guide that you can keep at your desk to quickly look up information on a given area when needed.

The author has worked in the CM field for many years and the constant challenge has always been shifting through the multitude of publications out there to 'get to the meat' of what he was looking for. It was out of this frustration that the book you are now reading was born.

This book puts the deluge of data about CM in an orderly arrangement along with footnotes citing the author's source, should the reader require further investigation of the topic.

On behalf of the Publisher, Burning Bulb Publishing, we appreciate your purchase of this book and hope you find it useful in planning and implementing CM in your organization.

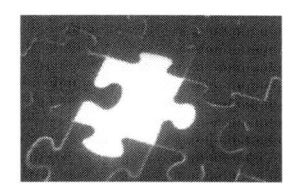

CHAPTER 1
WHAT IS CONFIGURATION MANAGEMENT?

Configuration Management (CM) is a field of management that focuses on establishing and maintaining consistency of a system's or product's performance and its functional and physical attributes with its requirements, design, and operational information throughout its life.[1]

To put it another way, CM is an administrative process that provides an organization with timely and accurate information about a product, system, etc., so that it can make consistent and correct decisions.

For information assurance, CM can be defined as the management of security features and assurances through control of changes made to hardware, software, firmware, documentation, test,

---

[1] MIL-HDBK-61A CONFIGURATION MANAGEMENT GUIDANCE 7 February 2001

test fixtures, and test documentation throughout the life cycle of an information system.[2]

Anatomically speaking, anything that exists, regardless if it is manmade or from nature, has a configuration.

A **configuration** is an arrangement of parts or elements.[3] Thus, the discipline of CM looks at such configurations and their individual parts (or configuration *items*.)

"The term **configuration item** (CI) refers to the fundamental structural unit of a configuration management system. Examples of CIs include individual requirements documents, software, models, plans, and people. Configuration Management systems oversee the life of the CIs through a combination of process and tools. The objective of these systems is to avoid the introduction of errors related to lack of testing or incompatibilities with other CIs."[4]

---

[2] National Information Systems Security Glossary
[3] http://www.thefreedictionary.com
[4] http://en.wikipedia.org/wiki/Configuration_item

The CM process encompasses:

- Configuration items
- Documents that define the performance, functional, and physical attributes of an item. These documents are referred to as configuration documentation.
- Other documents which are used for training, operation and maintenance of an item
- Associated and interfacing items that are used for training, operation, or maintenance of the configuration item.

The CM process is embodied in rules, procedures, techniques, methodology and resources to assure that:

- The configuration of the system and/or item (its attributes) is documented.
- Changes made to the item in the course of development, production and operation, are beneficial and are effected without adverse consequences.

CM should be considered a Tool for organizations. When used properly, it brings order to otherwise disorderly information.

Such order is accomplished through the use of standards, such as MIL-HDBK-61A, the Military Handbook on Configuration Management Guidance.

- Changes are managed until incorporated in all items affected.

The Need for CM

There were many reasons that CM came into existence and how effective CM is done within an organization determines how successful it will be. Most importantly, there existed a need to bring order to chaos.

Think about an automobile, for example. The engine alone contains many different components that are unique and specific to that make and model of vehicle. Could you imagine trying to assemble an engine for a 2009 Ford F-150 with parts from a 2007 Honda Accord? CM comes in to standardize the process and ensure that the correct product information is aligned with the product that is being developed.

According to MIL-HDBK-61A, "In the absence of CM, or where it is ineffectual, there may be:

- Equipment failures due to incorrect part installation or replacement;
- Schedule delays and increased cost due to unanticipated changes;
- Operational delays due to mismatches with support assets;
- Maintenance problems, downtime, and increased maintenance cost due to inconsistencies between equipment and its maintenance instructions; and,
- Numerous other circumstances

Can you imagine a world where CM didn't exist? Would you feel comfortable taking a flight knowing that the person who assembled the plane might not have known the 'configuration' of what he was working on?

CM's role in our world helps ensure the safety and reliability of entire industries, such as transportation.

> "A basic principle of management is that responsibility, unlike authority, cannot be delegated...nor can it be taken lightly."
> - MIL-HDBK-61A

which decrease operational effectiveness, and add cost.

"The severest consequence is catastrophic loss of expensive equipment and human life. Of course these failures may be attributed to causes other than poor CM. The point is that the intent of CM is to avoid cost and minimize risk.

"Those who consider the small investment in the CM process a cost-driver may not be considering the compensating benefits of CM and may be ignoring or underestimating the cost, schedule and technical risk of an inadequate or delayed CM process."

History of CM

The concepts of CM can be traced to the earliest of civilizations. The Seven Wonders of the Ancient World[5] are examples of engineering feats that would have required exceptional CM. *See following page for more information on CM applied to this temple.*[6]

Model of the Temple of Artemis, Istanbul, Turkey, one of the Seven Wonders of the Ancient World as defined by Antipatros Sidonios

---

[5] http://en.wikipedia.org/wiki/Temple_of_Artemis
[6] http://www.richeast.org/htwm/Greeks/wonders/temple.html

Configuration Management in Retrospect
The Temple of Artemis

"The Temple of Artemis was the third oldest wonder. It was built in 560 BCE to honor the Greek goddess Artemis on the site of an ancient shrine in Ephesus. It was also known as "the great marble temple" or "temple D". The construction of the Temple was funded by King Croesus of Lydia and it was designed by the Greek architect, Chersiphron. It was revolutionary in design and later became a model for Greek architects.

The Temple was said to have rivaled the Parthenon in size and fame. It measured 377 by 180 feet and had 106 columns, each measuring about 40 feet tall, which were placed in a double row around the center of the temple.

It was made from expensive and rare materials. The roof of the Temple was wholly constructed of planks of cedar. The Temple was made of marble and was ornamented inside and outside with gold, nearly overflowing with treasures."

The Industrial Revolution also relied on CM to move away from "one-of-a-kind" to mass production. However, the first use of the term "Configuration Management" was developed by the United States Department of Defense in the 1950s as a technical management discipline.

These concepts from the 1950s have been widely adopted by numerous technical management models. The following are some of the more common ones:

- Capability Maturity Model Integration (CMMI), *See Chapter 7*

- ISO 9000, *See Chapter 8*

- PRINCE2, *See Chapter 9*

- Information Technology Infrastructure Library (ITIL), *See Chapter 10*

- product lifecycle management, and

- application lifecycle management.

Many of these models have redefined configuration management from its traditional holistic approach to technical management.

Perceptions of Configuration Management

Organizations have verifying views (and approaches) to CM. Some treat CM as being similar to a librarian activity, and break out change control and change management as separate areas of discipline (as

Prince 2); some break out the traditional elements of revision control and engineering release into separate management disciplines; others treat CM as an overarching management discipline.

Military commands and contractors follow a very strict CM process that is documented in Military Standards (MIL-STDs).

Commercial entities might practice CM, but may refer to it as something else (possibly under the umbrella of Project Management or Data Management.)

Regardless of how CM is referred to from business to business, the most successful ones are those that implement CM practices as part of their operational model. These businesses apply technical and administrative direction to their products and processes. Through diligent observation of this work, they perform the following activities:

1. Document and identify a product's physical and functional features

2. Regulate changes to those features
3. Document any changes
4. Verify that requirements were met

Rising Popularity of CM

The Perry Initiative

In 1994, Secretary of Defense William Perry announced that one of the Department of Defense's (DoD's) top priorities would be to move away from military-unique specifications and standards (milspecs) and toward reliance upon private sector standards.[7]

> "Moving to greater use of performance and commercial specifications and standards is one of the most important actions that DoD must take to ensure we are able to meet our military, economic, and policy objectives in the future.
>
> "Federal, state and local governments and agencies have formally adopted thousands of voluntary standards produced by the ANSI Federation, and the process appears to be accelerating."
>
> - William Perry
> Former US Secretary of Defense

---

[7] http://www.ansi.org/government_affairs/laws_policies

ISO Guidelines

"Young people today find it difficult to imagine how far we were, at that time, from the global view that now seems so familiar. The earth was an archipelago of distinct worlds."

- Raymond Frontard, Former Director-General of AFNOR*

(*French Standardization Group and ISO participating member reflecting on the origins of ISO, from *Friendship Among Equals*)

The International Organization for Standardization (ISO) is the world's largest developer and publisher of International Standards that consists of a network of the national standards institutes of 162 countries, one member per country, with a Central Secretariat in Geneva, Switzerland, that coordinates the system.

ISO is a non-governmental organization that was founded in 1947 and forms a bridge between the public and private sectors, publishing over 16,500 international standards since inception.

On the one hand, many of its member institutes are part of the governmental structure of their countries, or are mandated by their government. On the other hand, other members have their roots uniquely in the private sector, having been set up by national partnerships of industry associations.

Therefore, ISO enables a consensus to be reached on solutions that meet both the requirements of business and the broader needs of society.[8]

The Software Engineering Institute
The Carnegie Mellon® Software Engineering Institute (SEI) is a federally funded research and development center. Founded in 1984, the SEI staff has advanced software engineering principles and practices and has served as a national resource in software engineering, computer security, and process improvement.[9]

SEI has recognized CM as a Key Process Area and have pioneered Compatibility Maturity Models (CMMs) to improve processes within an organization. The use of various CMMs led SEI to the creation of

---

[8] http://www.iso.org/iso/about.htm
[9] http://www.sei.cmu.edu/about/

CMM integration to sort out the problem of using multiple CMMs.[10] By combining the various CMMs into a singular improvement framework allowed business entities to pursue enterprise-wide process improvement.

CM Standards

The Federal Standardization Manual defines a Standard as a document that establishes uniform engineering and technical requirements for processes, procedures, practices and methods. Because most changes are evolutionary, the influence of Standards on most processes and products is pervasive.

Below is a list of the most common standards and guidelines currently used for CM:

Reference Number	Name
STANDARDS	
ANSI/EIA-649-1998	National Consensus Standard for Configuration Management
EIA-649-A 2004	National Consensus Standard for Configuration Management

---

[10] "CMMI: Guiidelines for Process Integration and Product Improvement," 2003, Pearson Education, Inc.

CHAPTER 1: What is Configuration Management? 25

EIA-836	Configuration Management Data Exchange and Interoperability
Federal Standard 1037C	Telecommunications: Glossary of Telecommunication Terms
GEIA Standard 836-2002	Configuration Management Data Exchange and Interoperability
IEEE Std. 828-1998	IEEE Standard for Software Configuration Management Plans
MIL-STD-973*	Configuration Management (*cancelled on September 20, 2000)
STANAG 4159	NATO Material Configuration Management Policy and Procedures for Multinational Joint Projects
STANAG 4427	Introduction of Allied Configuration Management Publications (ACMPs)
GUIDELINES	
ANSI/EIA-632-1998	Processes for Engineering a System
IEEE Std. 1042-1987	IEEE Guide to Software Configuration Management
ISO 10007	Quality management - Guidelines for configuration management
ISO/IEC 12207-1995	Information technology -- Software life cycle processes
MIL-HDBK-61A	Configuration Management Guidance
GEIA-HB-649	Implementation Guide for Configuration Management

Types of CM

There are different types of CM and it all relates to how information within a project is managed and controlled.

For the scope of this book, we will focus on the following three main categories:

- Software CM
- Hardware CM
- Enterprise CM

A chapter for each of the above categories has been dedicated in this book.

CHAPTER 2
CM Lifecycle Management

Figure 1 illustrates the Top Level CM Activity Model as defined by the US Dept. of Defense.[11] In this chapter, we will look at each step in this model and what roles are expected.

Management and Planning

Management begins with an authorization to create a CM Program. This entity will establish the organization, roles and responsibilities, assign representatives, training, and will aid in conflict resolution. Working relationships at this stage are established and breakout groups such as **Integrated Project Teams** (IPTs) are formed.

Planning here describes the identifying the vision of management, definition the mission of the CM Program, establishing policy, and conducting CM

---

[11] MIL-HDBK-61A (public domain)

28 CONFIGURATION MANAGEMENT

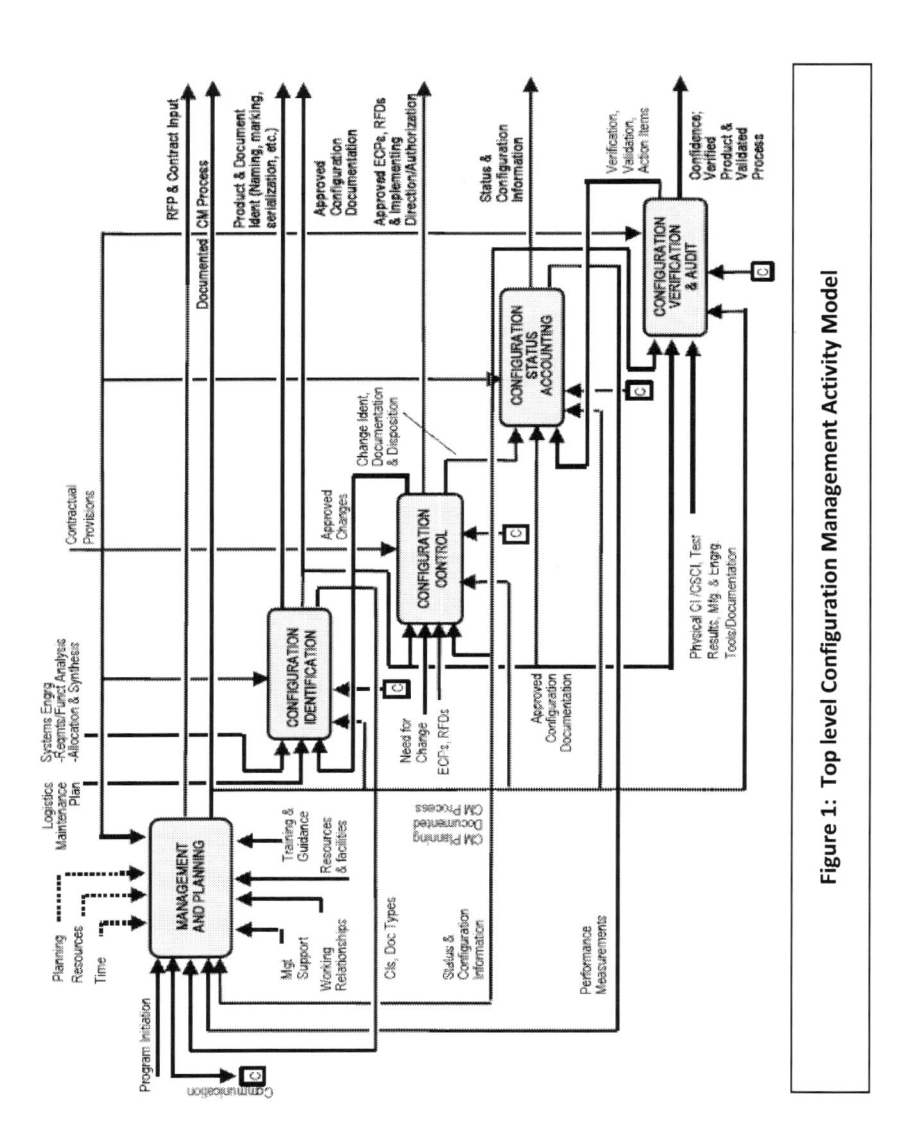

Figure 1: Top level Configuration Management Activity Model

risk analysis. During the Planning step, the CM system that will be used (CMMI, ITIL, etc.) is established.

It should be the goal of the Management and Planning step to tailor the project as necessary for continuous process improvement and provide status accounting on the CM Program's progress.

Configuration Identification

The **Configuration Identification** step provides the foundation for baseline identification and baseline management. In other words, this step identifies "what has been approved for concurrent use in the project, who owns the information, how information was approved for CM control, and the latest approved release."[12]

This step also identifies the document and drawing repository, how parts will be classified and any other aspects of inventory control.

---

[12] Little Book of Configuration Management, Nov. 1998

The use of automated systems (such as asset databases) and special-purpose data collection devices (such as bar code readers) will facilitate asset management.

It is important for organizations to know their assets' physical location, where they are assigned, who they are assigned to, and their status.

Establishing Configuration Baselines

Business assets can take the form of both hardware and software. For example, furniture, and office equipment are considered physical assets. These assets have a life cycle that spans acquisition, in-service, and disposal. It is CM's role to identify and manage them through their life cycle.

Usually, physical assets are assigned unique identifiers and labeled when acquired, managed and assigned a monetary value which generally depreciates while in-service, and disposed of once they become obsolete.

Computer hardware, software, and communications

components, as well as being important business tools, are valuable assets. They should be identified, tracked, and managed like any other company assets.

Performing an initial inventory of these assets will establish a configuration management baseline. If the information collected during the inventory is input to an automated asset management system, then technology assets can also be managed in a controlled manner. This increases the efficiency of the considerable effort spent installing or moving these components.[13]

Configuration Control

The **Configuration Control** step establishes interface management, asset accountability, the change process, who controls the baseline, what non-conformance items will be tracked, and how (or how often) something will be upgraded. This is done through input received from the Configuration Identification step.

---

[13] Establishing a Configuration Management Baseline, Craig Borysowich, Jan. 2007

Configuration Control step designates how much control each step will have. For example, what rights will the author have versus the project manager, etc. It also identifies what persons or groups will have the authority to make changes at each level.

Configuration Control creates the framework to develop an item or system with a known configuration that can be exactly reproduced.

Configuration Control allows for change decisions to be based on knowledge of what the change will impact.

Configuration Status Accounting

Configuration Status Accounting (CSA) is the recording and reporting of information needed to manage configuration items effectively, including:

- A record of the approved configuration documentation and identification numbers.
- The status of proposed changes, deviations, and waivers to the configuration.
- The implementation status of approved changes.
- The configuration of all units of the configuration item in the

operational inventory.

- Discrepancies from Functional and Physical configuration audits.[14]

Configuration and Verification Audit

The **Configuration and Verification Audit** step evaluates the content, baseline integrity, and release integrity of all controlled products to ensure that they conform to their configuration documents.

"Inputs to Configuration Verification and Audit (Functional and Physical Configuration Audit) include: schedule information (from status accounting), configuration

CSA information is typically maintained in a CM database. This can include items such as the as-designed, as-built, as-delivered, or as-modified configuration of any serial-numbered unit of the product as well as of any replaceable component within the product.

Other information, such as the current status or change history of any change can also be accessed in the database.

---

[14] http://nawctsd.navair.navy.mil/Resources/Library/Acqguide/ch6cm.htm

> Configuration verification should be considered a function of the when creating or modifying a product.
>
> This should be validated by the principal stakeholders.

documentation (from configuration identification), product test results, and the physical hardware or software product or its representation, manufacturing instructions, and the software engineering environment.

"Outputs are verification that (1) the product's performance requirements have been achieved by the product design and (2) the product design has been accurately documented in the configuration documentation. This process is also applied to verify the incorporation of approved engineering changes.

"Successful completion of verification and audit activities results in a verified product and documentation set that may be confidently considered a Product

Baseline, as well as a validated process that will maintain the continuing consistency of product to documentation."[15]

---

[15] MIL-HDBK-61A

CONFIGURATION MANAGEMENT

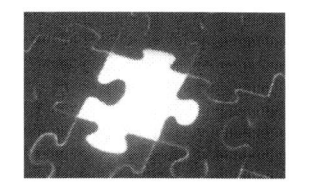

CHAPTER 3
Software Configuration Management

As mentioned in Chapter 1, the success of a project is largely dependent on how effective it implements CM. CM becomes more important as the size of software increases within an organization.

CM is needed to allow team members to work together in a controlled environment while maintaining the flexibility they need to accomplish their work.

The traditional software configuration management (SCM) process is looked upon as the best solution to handling changes in software projects. It identifies the functional and physical attributes of software at various points in time, and performs systematic control of changes to the identified attributes for the purpose of maintaining software integrity and traceability throughout the software development life cycle.

The SCM process further defines the need to trace changes, and the ability to verify that the final delivered software has all of the planned enhancements that are supposed to be included in the release. It identifies four procedures that must be defined for each software project to ensure that a sound SCM process is implemented. They are:

- Configuration identification
- Configuration change control
- Configuration status accounting
- Configuration audits

These terms and definitions change from standard to standard, but are essentially the same. An additional list of definitions from MIL-HDBK-61A can be found in APPENDIX B of this book. Implementing CM best practices is critical to how well a software product is developed and maintained.

Configuration identification is the process of identifying the attributes that define every aspect of a configuration item. A configuration item is a product (hardware and/or software) that has an end-user purpose. These attributes are recorded in configuration documentation and baselined. Baselining an attribute forces formal configuration change control processes to be effected in the event that these attributes are changed.

Configuration change control is a set of processes and approval stages required to change a configuration item's attributes and to re-baseline them.

Configuration status accounting is the ability to record and report on the configuration baselines associated with each configuration item at any moment of time.

Configuration audits are broken into functional and physical configuration audits. They occur either at delivery or at the moment of effecting the change. A functional configuration audit ensures that functional and performance attributes of a configuration item are achieved, while a physical configuration audit ensures that a configuration item is installed in accordance with the requirements of its detailed design documentation.

CM is widely used by many military organizations to manage the technical aspects of any complex systems, such as weapon systems, vehicles, and information systems. The discipline combines the capability aspects that these systems provide an organization with the issues of management of change to these systems over time.

Outside of the military, CM is equally appropriate to a wide range of fields and industry and commercial sectors.[16]

---

[16] ANSI/EIA-649-1998 National Consensus Standard for Configuration Management

CHAPTER 4
Hardware Configuration Management

Computer hardware configuration management (HCM) is the process of creating and maintaining an up-to-date record of all the components of the infrastructure, including related documentation. Its purpose is to show what makes up the infrastructure and illustrate the physical locations and links between each item, which are known as configuration items.

The scope of HCM is assumed to include, at a minimum, all configuration items used in the provision of live, operational services.

Computer hardware configuration management provides direct control over information technology (IT) assets and improves the ability of the service provider to deliver quality IT services in an economical and effective manner.

Computer hardware configuration goes beyond the recording of computer hardware for the purpose of asset management, although it can be used to maintain asset information.

The extra value provided is the rich source of support information that it provides to all interested parties. This information is typically stored together in a configuration management database (CMDB).

HCM should work closely with change management.

The CMDB

A configuration management database (CMDB) is a repository of information related to all the components of an information system. Although repositories similar to CMDBs have been used by IT departments for many years, the term CMDB stems from ITIL (Information Technology Infrastructure Library).

In the ITIL context, a CMDB represents the authorized configuration of the significant components of the IT environment. A key goal of a CMDB is to help an organization understand the relationships between these components and track their configuration. The CMDB is a fundamental component of the ITIL framework's Configuration Management process. CMDB implementations often involve integration with other systems, such as Asset Management Systems. These integrations may make use of either a real-time, federated design or an ETL (extract, transform, load) solution.[17]

All components of the IT infrastructure should be registered in the CMDB. The responsibilities of configuration management with regard to the CMDB are:

- identification
- control
- status accounting
- verification

The scope of configuration management is assumed to include:

---

[17] Office of Government Commerce (OGC), ed.: Service Support. IT Infrastructure Library (ITIL).

- physical client and server hardware products and versions
- operating system software products and versions
- application development software products and versions
- technical architecture product sets and versions as they are defined and introduced
- live documentation
- networking products and versions
- live application products and versions
- definitions of packages of software releases
- definitions of hardware base configurations
- configuration item standards and definitions

The benefits of computer hardware configuration management are:

- helps to minimize the impact of changes
- provides accurate information on CIs
- improves security by controlling the versions of CIs in use
- facilitates adherence to legal obligations
- helps in financial and expenditure planning

CHAPTER 5
Enterprise Configuration Management

The information contained in this chapter is based on the Object-oriented Process, Environment, and Notation (OPEN). OPEN is a free, public domain, industry-standard approach for the production of endeavor-specific development methods. OPEN was originally created in the mid-1990s as a merger of several earlier object-oriented software development methods, especially MOSES by Brian Henderson-Sellers, SOMA by Ian Graham, ADM3 by Firesmith, and Synthesis by Meilir Page-Jones. Since then, OPEN has grown and evolved to support the development, sustainment, and retirement of software-intensive systems as well as to support business [re]engineering.

Enterprise Configuration Management is the configuration management activity consisting of the cohesive collection of all tasks that are primarily performed to manage an enterprise's baselines of configuration items.[18]

Responsibilities

The typical responsibilities of Enterprise Configuration Management are to:

- Ensure that stakeholders know the major components of the enterprise.

---
[18] http://www.opfro.org

- Minimize project disruption due to uncontrolled changes to major components of the enterprise.
- Provide an audit trail on why, when, and by whom baselined work products are changed.
- Identify configuration items and baselines to enable the retrieval of specific versions of work products and baselines.
- Control changes to configuration items and baselines to minimize enterprise disruption.
- Report the status of changes to configuration items and baselines to all relevant stakeholders.
- Audit baselines to ensure that they consist of the correct versions of the correct configuration items.

Preconditions

Configuration Management typically may begin when the following conditions hold:

- The endeavor is started.
- The configuration management team, change control board, and enterprise team are:
  - Initially staffed.
  - Adequately trained in configuration management.

Tasks

Enterprise Configuration Management typically involves the following teams performing the following tasks in an iterative, incremental, parallel, and time-boxed manner:

- Configuration Management Team, which performs:
    - Configuration Management Planning
    - Configuration Identification
    - Version Control
    - Configuration Control
    - Configuration Status Reporting
    - Configuration Auditing
- Change Control Board, which performs:
    - Configuration Control
- Enterprise Team, which performs:
    - Version Control

Environments

Enterprise Configuration Management is typically performed using the following environment(s) and associated tools:

- Reuse Environment:
    - Configuration Management Tool
    - Problem Reporting Tool

- Development Environments:
  - Configuration Management Tool
  - Problem Reporting Tool
- Test Environment:
  - Configuration Management Tool
  - Problem Reporting Tool
- Production Environments:
  - Configuration Management Tool
  - Problem Reporting Tool

Work Products

Enterprise Configuration Management typically results in the production of all or part of the following work products in the configuration management work product set:

- Configuration Management Plan
- Change Request Form
- Configuration Identification Report
- Configuration Control Board Meeting Minutes
- Configuration Status Report
- Configuration Audit Report

CHAPTER 5: Enterprise Configuration Management | 49

Phases

Enterprise Configuration Management tasks are typically performed during the following phases:

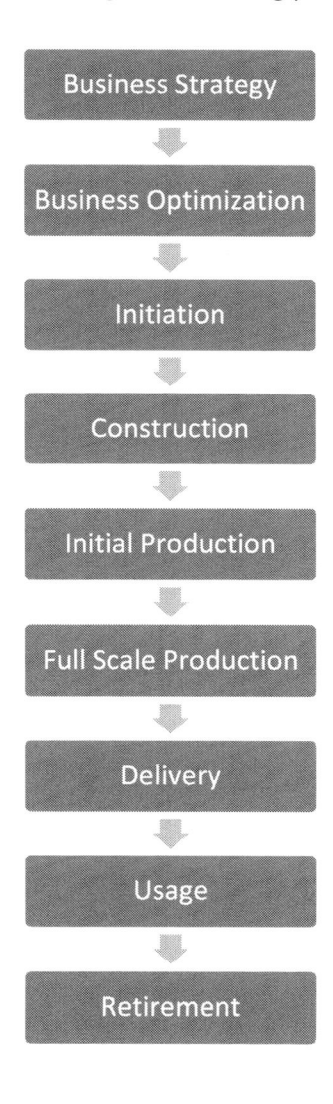

- Business Strategy
- Business Optimization
- Initiation
- Construction
- Initial Production
- Full Scale Production
- Delivery
- Usage
- Retirement

Business Strategy Phase

The **Business Strategy Phase** is the first phase of the business engineering cycle during which the development organization develops new strategies and architectures for all or part of the customer organization's business enterprise.

Goals

The typical goals of the Business Strategy Phase of a business engineering project are to:

- Reach a consensus regarding the new operating vision and mission of the reengineered business enterprise.
- Develop the associated new business strategies and architectures for the reengineered business enterprise.
- Develop a framework for deploying new business capabilities.
- Plan the implementation of (and transition to) this new reengineered business enterprise.

Objectives

To meet these goals, the typical objectives of the business strategy phase on a business engineering project are to:

- Analyze the customer organization, marketplace, relevant technologies, and user organizations to create a basis for reengineering the business enterprise.
- Develop a new vision of the reengineered business enterprise:
    - Strategic direction
    - Mission
    - Value proposition for users, shareholders, and employees
- Develop appropriate business strategies for dealing with:
    - New target markets and customer organizations
    - Appropriate new products, services, and associated pricing models
    - New delivery channels for these products and services

- o New or improved business capabilities to supply these products and services
- o New and updated applications to support these business capabilities
- o Relevant technologies to be used in these applications
- o New relationships with vendors and partners to support these business capabilities, applications, and technologies
- Develop initial new architectures (i.e., business model) for the reengineered business enterprise:
  - o Business Object Model (BOM)
  - o Business Process Model
  - o Business Organizational Model
- Develop the business case for implementing the new business strategies and architectures:
  - o Estimate the benefits.
  - o Estimate the costs.
  - o Estimate the required resources.
  - o Estimate the required schedule.

- o Document the business case.
- Create a transition plan for successfully reengineering the business enterprise.
- Eliminate the highest project risks.

Business Optimization Phase

The **Business Optimization Phase** is the first phase of the business engineering cycle during which the development organization helps the customer organization optimize all or part of its business enterprise by implementing, communicating, and continually optimizing its new business strategies and architectures

Goals

The typical goals of the Business Optimization Phase of a business engineering project include:

- Implement the new business strategies by making the required and architected changes to the business enterprise.
- Continually optimize the business as business conditions change.

- Eliminate the highest project risks.

Objectives

To meet these goals, the typical objectives of the business optimization phase on a business engineering project include:

- Construct/reengineer the components of the customer's business (e.g., applications, facilities, organizations).
- Develop and deliver the brand and business communication plans.

Initiation Phase

The **Initiation Phase** is the first phase of the application development and life cycles during which enough of the application's requirements and architecture are produced so that agreement can be reached between the development organization and the customer organization regarding the goals and scope of the following phases.

Goals

The typical goals of the Initiation Phase of an application development project are to:

- Ensure that the development organization and the customer organization reach an early consensus regarding the customer organization's vision of the application.
- Ensure that critical decisions are early regarding technology, partnering, vendors, etc.
- Ensure that the development organization has plans for successfully producing the next version of the application.
- Estimate the cost and required schedule to the following construction and delivery phases.
- Eliminate the highest project risks.

Objectives

To meet these goals, the typical objectives of the initiation phase on an application development project are to:

- Obtain major stakeholder agreement on the customer's vision of the application.
- Engineer all high risk and architecturally-significant system requirements.
- Document the initial partial (e.g., 80%) system architecture (including major COTS component selection).
- Produce an architectural prototype consisting of:
    - The implementation of at least one end-to-end use case path.
    - A partial implementation of the domain layer.
- Produce a low-fidelity prototype of the user interface.
- Derive a realistic estimate of the scope of the current version of the application.
- Document appropriate plans for one or more of the following phases.

Construction Phase

In the **Construction Phase** the application development cycle phase during which the development organization completes construction of the single initial version of an system and its associated deliverable work products

Goals

The typical goals of the Construction Phase are to:

- Complete the construction of the initial current version of the system.
- Ready it for initial:
    - Delivery to the customer organization.
    - Deployment to the production environments.
    - Usage by the user organization(s).
- Thereby prepare for the following delivery phase.

Objectives

To meet these goals, the typical objectives of the construction phase are to:

- Complete the associated tasks of the following activities:
    - Requirements Engineering.
    - Architecting.
    - Design.
    - Implementation.
    - Testing (except for launch testing).
- Ensure that the application fulfills its specified requirements:
    - Operational requirements.
    - Quality requirements.
    - Informational requirements.
    - External API requirements.
    - Design constraints.
- Ensure that the application conforms to its documented system architecture including:
    - Database architecture.
    - Hardware architecture.
    - Information architecture.
    - Software architecture.
    - User interface architecture.

- Complete all associated work products (especially development documentation).
- Minimize the associated project:
  - Costs.
  - Schedule.
  - Risks.
- Determine if the application should be delivered (i.e., advance to the next phase) or be abandoned (e.g., due to major changes in market trends, major changes in the business' mission, or cost and schedule overruns).

Initial Production Phase

The **Initial Production Phase** is during which the initial small number of systems are manufactured

Goals

The typical goals of the Initial Production Phase of an application development project include:

- Manufacture a small initial number of systems to identify potential problems.
- Eliminate the highest risks before full scale production starts.

Full-Scale Production Phase

In the **Full-Scale Production Phase,** the systems are manufactured at a maximum rate.

Goals

The typical goal of the Full-Scale Production Phase of a development project is to maximize the rate of manufacture of the systems.

Delivery Phase

During the **Delivery Phase,** the development organization delivers one or more copies of the application to the customer organization and places them into use by the user organizations

Goals

The typical goals of the Delivery Phase of a development project include:

- Deliver the system to the customer organization.
- Place the completed and tested system into use by the user organizations.
- Eliminate the highest project risks.

Objectives

To meet these goals, the typical objectives of the delivery phase on an application development project include:

- Establish the data center
- Install and configure the production environment.
- Deploy the application to the production environment and tune its performance.
- Develop and deliver the delivery phase documentation.
- Perform and pass launch testing.
- Place the application into usage by the user organizations.
- Formally deliver the application to the customer organization.

Usage Phase

In the **Usage Phase,** the latest version of the application is used by members of the user organizations.

Goals

The typical goals of the usage phase of an application life project include:

- Keep the application functioning successfully until the next major upgrade or retirement.
- Eliminate the endeavor's highest risks.

Objectives

- To meet these goals, the typical objectives of the usage phase include:
- Perform Content Management tasks.
- Perform Operations tasks.
- Perform Maintenance (defect fixes and minor enhancements) tasks.
- Perform User Support tasks.

Retirement Phase

During the **Retirement Phase,** the application is retired from use and its components are either disposed of or else archived for future use.

Goals

The typical goal of the Retirement Phase is to take an application out of service.

Objectives

- To meet the above goals, the objectives of the retirement phase are to:
- Cease operations/usage in an orderly manner.
- Retire any associated documentation.
- Retire any associated data, hardware, and software components.

Enterprise Configuration Management Guidelines

The Enterprise CM activity is documented using the typical configuration for significant enterprises. It is intended to be configured (i.e., instantiated, extended, and tailored) to meet the needs of specific enterprises.

The preconditions of this activity should be the union of the preconditions of its constituent tasks.

The completion criteria for this activity should be the union of the post conditions of its constituent tasks.

CHAPTER 6
Establishing a CM Program

The CM Program

Establishing a CM Program in your environment requires a planned approach. The following are key elements that will need to be implemented:

1. Create a **CM Plan** to document the requirements, activities, and responsibilities of your Program.
2. Establish a high level process that contains milestones (also known as quality assurance 'gates') at which you can evaluate the integrity of your product.
3. Evaluate and institute tools that can support the needs of your process. Note: these tools should **not** require much (if any) modification 'out of the box.'
4. Create a configuration identification workflow that will be incorporated for all developed products under CM control.
5. Develop a plan/procedure to collect, record, process and maintain information that will be needed for configuration status accounting.

6. Develop a model to gauge how well the process is working and how quality improvements will be adopted into the process in the future.
7. Establish at what points in the process that budget will be evaluated to determine if the project that you are working on is within budget or not.
8. Create a CM Library that will house the CM Baseline, establish a Data Management Group, and any artifacts that make up the product's baseline.
9. Establish a Change Control Board (also known as an Engineering Review Board or Technical Review Board) that has the authority to manage the project's baselines.
10. Determine how audits will be handled (and how often).
11. Determine how archiving, storage, emergency backups, etc. will be handled. This includes creating a schedule of when and where the activity will take place.

The CM Plan

This following is an outline to help you construct your CM Plan.[19]

---

[19] "Configuration Management Plans: The Beginning to your CM Solution," July 1993, CMU/SEI-93-TR

Your CM Plan should contain the following sections:

1.0 INTRODUCTION

    1.1 Purpose

    1.2 Scope

    1.3 Definitions

    1.4 References

    1.5 Tailoring

2.0 CONFIGURATION MANAGEMENT

    2.1 Organization

    2.2 Responsibilities

    2.3 Relationship of CM to the process life cycle

        2.3.1 Interfaces to other organizations on the project

        2.3.2 Other project organizations CM responsibilities

3.0 CONFIGURATION MANAGEMENT ACTIVITIES

3.1 Configuration Identification

3.1.1 Specification Identification

- Labeling and numbering scheme for documents and files

- How identification between documents and files relate

- Description of identification tracking scheme

- When a document/file identification number enters controlled status

- How the identification scheme addresses versions and releases

- How the identification scheme addresses hardware, application software system software, COTS products, support software (e.g., test data and files), etc.

3.1.2 Change Control Form Identification

- Numbering scheme for each of the forms used

3.1.3 Project Baselines

- Identify various baselines for the project
- For each baseline created provide the following information:
  - How and when it is created
  - Who authorizes and who verifies it
  - The purpose
  - What goes into it (software and documentation)

3.1.4 Library

- Identification and control mechanisms used
- Number of libraries and the types
- Backup and disaster plans and procedures
- Recovery process for any type of loss

- Retention policies and procedures
- What needs to be retained, for who, and for how long
- How is the information retained (on-line, off-line, media type and format)

3.2 Configuration Control

3.2.1 Procedures for changing baselines (procedures may vary with each baseline)

3.2.2 Procedures for processing change requests and approvals- change classification scheme

- Change reporting documentation
- Change control flow diagram

3.2.3 Organizations assigned responsibilities for change control

3.2.4 Change Control Boards (CCBs) - describe and provide the following information for each:

- Charter
- Members
- Role
- Procedures
- Approval mechanisms

3.2.5 Interfaces, overall hierarchy, and the responsibility for communication between multiple CCBs, when applicable

3.2.6 Level of control - identify how it will change throughout the life cycle, when applicable

3.2.7 Document revisions - how they will be handled

3.2.8 Automated tools used to perform change control

3.3 Configuration Status Accounting

3.3.1 Storage, handling and release of project media

3.3.2 Types of information needed to be reported and the control over this information that is needed

3.3.3 Reports to be produced (e.g., management reports, QA reports, CCB reports) and who the audience is for each and the information needed to produce each report

3.3.4 Release process, to include the following information:

- What is in the release
- Who the release is being provided to and when
- The media the release is on
- Any known problems in the release
- Any known fixes in the release
- Installation instructions

3.3.5 Document status accounting and change management status accounting that needs to occur

3.4 Configuration Auditing

3.4.1 Number of audits to be done and when they will be done (internal audits as well as configuration audits); for each audit provide the following:

- Which baseline it is tied to, if applicable
- Who performs the audit
- What is audited
- What is the CM role in the audit, and what are the roles of other organizations in the audit
- How formal is the audit

3.4.2 All reviews that CM supports; for each provide the following:

- The materials to be reviewed
- CM responsibility in the review and the responsibilities of other organizations

4.0 CM MILESTONES

- Define all CM project milestones (e.g., baselines, reviews, audits)
- Describe how the CM milestones tie into the software development process
- Identify what the criteria are for reaching each milestone

5.0 TRAINING

- Identify the kinds and amounts of training (e.g., orientation, tools)

6.0 SUBCONTRACTOR/VENDOR SUPPORT

- Describe any subcontractor and/or vendor support and interfacing, if applicable

CM Best Practices

By building and maintaining configuration management best-practices, you can expect several benefits. Below are some things to keep in mind:

- Involve everyone in the CM process
- Create an environment that facilitates good CM
- Define and document your CM process
- Incorporate a tool that automates your process
- Ensure that your employees have the technical background to understand the

task at hand and what is required from a CM prospective for compliance and documentation support

- Create the CM Plan and procedures at the beginning stages of a project and ensure they are included in the strategy of the project

The CM process is supported by a system. This system can be documented in a CM *system performance specification*.

This specification is part of the output from the CM planning activity.

Key functionality, selected tools, interfaces, and tool capabilities should also be documented and kept current.

76 CONFIGURATION MANAGEMENT

Typical CM Organization Structure

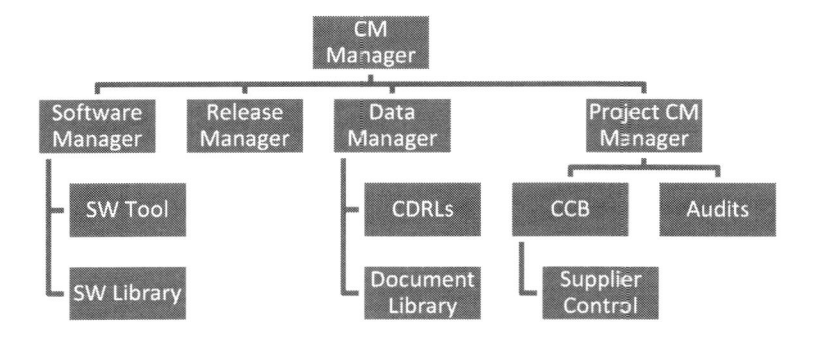

```
                        CM
                      Manager
    ┌──────────┬─────────┴────────┬──────────────┐
 Software    Release           Data          Project CM
 Manager     Manager          Manager         Manager
    │                            │          ┌─────┴─────┐
    ├─ SW Tool                   ├─ CDRLs   CCB       Audits
    │                            │           │
    └─ SW Library                └─ Document └─ Supplier
                                    Library     Control
```

Program Phasing and Milestones

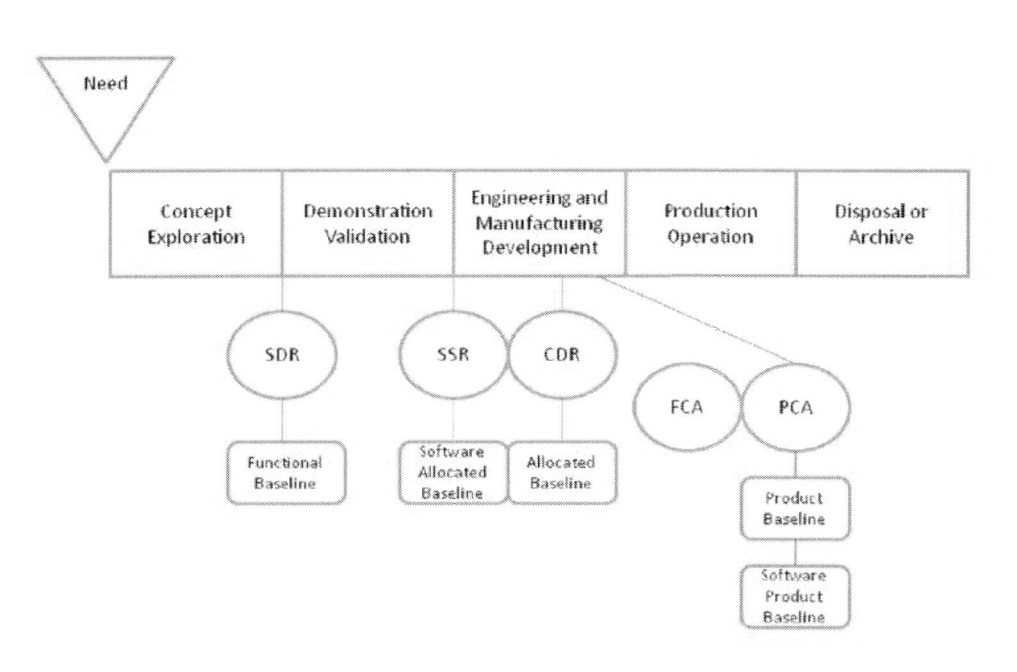

Need

| Concept Exploration | Demonstration Validation | Engineering and Manufacturing Development | Production Operation | Disposal or Archive |

- SDR → Functional Baseline
- SSR → Software Allocated Baseline
- CDR → Allocated Baseline
- FCA
- PCA → Product Baseline → Software Product Baseline

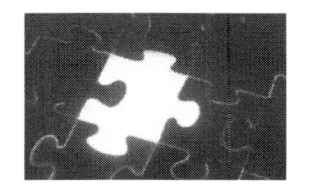

CHAPTER 7
CMMI

Capability Maturity Model Integration

Capability Maturity Model Integration (CMMI) in software engineering and organizational development is a process improvement approach that provides organizations with the essential elements for effective process improvement. It can be used to guide process improvement across a project, a division, or an entire organization.

CMMI can help integrate traditionally separate organizational functions, set process improvement goals and priorities, provide guidance for quality processes, and provide a point of reference for appraising current processes.[20]

---

[20] What is CMMI?. Software Engineering Institute. 10/30/2008

CONFIGURATION MANAGEMENT

Characteristics of the Maturity levels

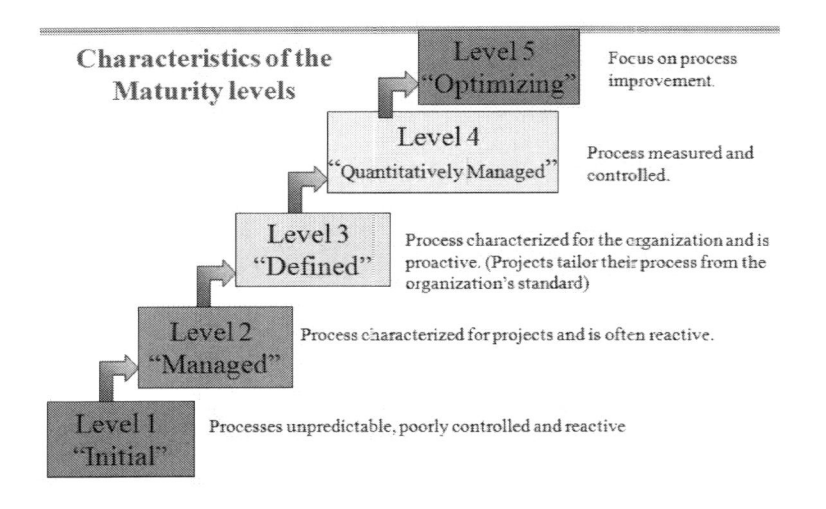

- **Level 5 "Optimizing"** — Focus on process improvement.
- **Level 4 "Quantitatively Managed"** — Process measured and controlled.
- **Level 3 "Defined"** — Process characterized for the organization and is proactive. (Projects tailor their process from the organization's standard)
- **Level 2 "Managed"** — Process characterized for projects and is often reactive.
- **Level 1 "Initial"** — Processes unpredictable, poorly controlled and reactive

Characteristics of the Maturity Levels[21]

Overview

CMMI is a collection of best practices that meet the needs of organizations in different areas of interest. A collection of best practices that cover a particular area of interest is called a CMMI model.

CMMI currently addresses three areas of interest:

1. Product and service development — CMMI for Development (CMMI-DEV),
2. Service establishment, management, and delivery — CMMI for Services (CMMI-SVC), and

---

[21] Sally Godfrey (2008) What is CMMI?. NASA presentation.

3. Product and service acquisition — CMMI for Acquisition (CMMI-ACQ).

CMMI was developed by a group of experts from industry, government, and the Software Engineering Institute (SEI) at Carnegie Mellon University. CMMI models provide guidance for developing or improving processes that meet the business goals of an organization. A CMMI model may also be used as a framework for appraising the process maturity of the organization.

CMMI originated in software engineering but has been highly generalized over the years to embrace other areas of interest, such as the development of hardware products, the delivery of all kinds of services, and the acquisition of products and services. The word "software" does not appear in definitions of CMMI. This generalization of improvement concepts makes CMMI extremely abstract. It is not as specific to software engineering as its predecessor, the Software CMM (CMM, see below).

CONFIGURATION MANAGEMENT

CMMI is the successor of the Capability Maturity Model (CMM) or Software CMM. The CMM was developed from 1987 until 1997. In 2002, CMMI Version 1.1 was released. Version 1.2 followed in August 2006.

History

Capability Maturity Model Integration (CMMI) is developed by the CMMI project, which aimed to improve the usability of maturity models by integrating many different models into one framework. The project consisted of members of industry, government and the Carnegie Mellon Software Engineering Institute (SEI). The main sponsors included the Office of the Secretary of Defense (OSD) and the National Defense Industrial Association.

CMMI topics

CMMI representation

CMMI exists in two representations: continuous and staged. The continuous representation is designed to allow the user to focus on the specific processes that are considered important for the organization's immediate business objectives, or those to which the organization assigns a high degree of risk. The staged representation is designed to provide a standard sequence of improvements, and can serve as a basis for comparing the maturity of different projects and organizations. The staged representation also provides for an easy migration from the SW-CMM to CMMI.

CMMI Model Framework

Depending on the CMMI constellation (acquisition, services, development) you use, the process areas it contains will vary. Key process areas are the areas that will be covered by the organization's processes. The table below lists the process areas that are present in all CMMI constellations. This collection of sixteen process areas is called the CMMI Model Framework, or CMF.

Capability Maturity Model Integration (CMMI) Model Framework (CMF)

Abbreviation	Name	Area	Maturity Level
REQM	Requirements Management	Engineering	2
PMC	Project Monitoring and Control	Project Management	2
PP	Project Planning	Project Management	2
CM	Configuration Management	Support	2
MA	Measurement and Analysis	Support	2
PPQA	Process and Product Quality Assurance	Support	2

OPD	Organizational Process Definition	Process Management	3
OPF	Organizational Process Focus	Process Management	3
OT	Organizational Training	Process Management	3
IPM	Integrated Project Management	Project Management	3
RSKM	Risk Management	Project Management	3
DAR	Decision Analysis and Resolution	Support	3
OPP	Organizational Process Performance	Process Management	4
QPM	Quantitative Project Management	Project Management	4
OID	Organizational Innovation and Deployment	Process Management	5

| CAR | Causal Analysis and Resolution | Support | 5 |

CMMI models

CMMI best practices are published in documents called models, each of which addresses a different area of interest. The current release of CMMI, version 1.2, provides models for three areas of interest: development, acquisition, and services.

- CMMI for Development (CMMI-DEV), v1.2 was released in August 2006. It addresses product and service development processes.
- CMMI for Acquisition (CMMI-ACQ), v1.2 was released in November 2007. It addresses supply chain management, acquisition, and outsourcing processes in government and industry.
- CMMI for Services (CMMI-SVC), v1.2 was released in February 2009. It addresses guidance for delivering services within an organization and to external customers.

Regardless of which model an organization chooses, CMMI best practices should be adapted by an organization according to its business objectives.

Appraisal

An organization cannot be certified in CMMI; instead, an organization is appraised. Depending on the type of appraisal, the organization can be awarded a maturity level rating (1-5) or a capability level achievement profile.

Many organizations find value in measuring their progress by conducting an appraisal. Appraisals are typically conducted for one or more of the following reasons:

1. To determine how well the organization's processes compare to CMMI best practices, and to identify areas where improvement can be made
2. To inform external customers and suppliers of how well the organization's processes compare to CMMI best practices

3. To meet the contractual requirements of one or more customers

Appraisals of organizations using a CMMI model[22] must conform to the requirements defined in the Appraisal Requirements for CMMI (ARC) document. There are three classes of appraisals, A, B and C, which focus on identifying improvement opportunities and comparing the organization's processes to CMMI best practices. Appraisal teams use a CMMI model and ARC-conformant appraisal method to guide their evaluation of the organization and their reporting of conclusions. The appraisal results can then be used (e.g., by a process group) to plan improvements for the organization.

The Standard CMMI Appraisal Method for Process Improvement (SCAMPI) is an appraisal method that meets all of the ARC requirements.[23]

---

[22] For the latest published CMMI appraisal results see the SEI Web site

[23] Standard CMMI Appraisal Method for Process Improvement (SCAMPISM) A, Version 1.2: Method Definition Document". CMU/SEI-2006-HB-002. Software Engineering Institute. 2006.

A Class A appraisal is more formal and is the only one that can result in a level rating. Results of an appraisal may be published (if the appraised organization approves) on the CMMI Web site of the SEI: Published SCAMPI Appraisal Results. SCAMPI also supports the conduct of ISO/IEC 15504, also known as SPICE (Software Process Improvement and Capability Determination), assessments etc.

Achieving CMMI compliance

The traditional approach that organizations often adopt to achieve compliance with the CMMI involves the establishment of an Engineering Process Group (EPG) and Process Action Teams (PATs)[24] This approach requires that members of the EPG and PATs be trained in the CMMI, that an informal (SCAMPI C) appraisal be performed, and that process areas be prioritized for improvement. More modern approaches that involve the deployment of commercially available, CMMI-compliant processes, can significantly reduce the time to achieve compliance. SEI has maintained statistics on the "time to move up" for organizations

---

[24] http://www.sei.cmu.edu/cmmi/adoption/cmmi-start.html

adopting the earlier Software CMM and primarily using the traditional approach.[25] These statistics indicate that, since 1987, the median times to move from Level 1 to Level 2 is 23 months, and from Level 2 to Level 3 is an additional 20 months. These statistics have not been updated for the CMMI.

The Software Engineering Institute's (SEI) Team Software Process methodology and the Capability Maturity Modeling framework have been successfully employed to accelerate progress from Maturity Level 1 to Maturity Level 4. They've demonstrated progressing from Level 1 to Level 4 in 30 months, which is less than half of the average time it has taken traditionally.[26]

Applications

The SEI published that 60 organizations measured increases of performance in the categories of cost, schedule, productivity, quality and customer satisfaction.[27] The median increase in performance varied between 14% (customer satisfaction) and 62% (productivity).

---

[25] http://www.sei.cmu.edu/appraisal-program/profile/pdf/SW-CMM/2006marSwCMM.pdf
[26] http://www.sei.cmu.edu/pub/documents/05.reports/pdf/05sr012.pdf
[27] http://www.sei.cmu.edu/publications/documents/06.reports/06tr004.html

However, the CMMI model mostly deals with what processes should be implemented, and not so much with how they can be implemented. These results do not guarantee that applying CMMI will increase performance in every organization. A small company with few resources may be less likely to benefit from CMMI; this view is supported by the Process Maturity Profile (page 10). Of the small organizations (<25 employees), 70.5% are assessed at level 2: Managed, while 52.8% of the organizations with 1001–2000 employees are rated at the highest level (5: Optimizing).

Interestingly, Turner & Jain (2002) argue that although it is obvious there are large differences between CMMI and agile methods, both approaches have much in common. They believe neither way is the 'right' way to develop software, but that there are phases in a project where one of the two is better suited. They suggest one should combine the different fragments of the methods into a new hybrid method. Sutherland et al. (2007) assert that a combination of Scrum and CMMI brings more adaptability and predictability than either one alone.

David J. Anderson (2005) gives hints on how to interpret CMMI in an agile manner. Other viewpoints about using CMMI and Agile development are available on the SEI Web site.

The combination of the project management technique Earned value management (EVM) with CMMI has been described (Solomon, 2002). To conclude with a similar use of CMMI, Extreme Programming (XP), a software engineering method, has been evaluated with CMM/CMMI (Nawrocki et al., 2002). For example, the XP requirements management approach, (which relies on oral communication), was evaluated as not compliant with CMMI.

CMMI can be appraised using two different approaches: staged and continuous. The staged approach yields appraisal results as one of five maturity levels. The continuous approach yields one of six capability levels. The differences in these approaches are felt only in the appraisal; the best practices are equivalent and result in equivalent process improvement results.

Capability Maturity Model – Integrated

Level	Focus	Process Areas	Result
5 Optimizing	*Continuous process improvement*	Organizational Innovation & Deployment Causal Analysis and Resolution	Productivity & Quality
4 Quantitatively Managed	*Quantitative management*	Organizational Process Performance Quantitative Project Management	
3 Defined	*Process standardization*	Requirements Development Technical Solution Product Integration Verification Validation Organizational Process Focus Organizational Process Definition Organizational Training Integrated Project Management Risk Management Decision Analysis and Resolution	
2 Managed	*Basic project management*	Requirements Management Project Planning Project Monitoring & Control Supplier Agreement Management Measurement and Analysis Process & Product Quality Assurance Configuration Management	
1 Initial	*Competent people and heroics*		

CHAPTER 8
ISO 9000

ISO 9000 is a family of standards for quality management systems. ISO 9000 is maintained by ISO, the International Organization for Standardization and is administered by accreditation and certification bodies. The rules are updated, as the requirements motivate changes over time.

Some of the requirements in ISO 9001:2008 (which is one of the standards in the ISO 9000 family) include

- a set of procedures that cover all key processes in the business;
- monitoring processes to ensure they are effective;
- keeping adequate records;
- checking output for defects, with appropriate and corrective action where necessary;
- regularly reviewing individual processes and the quality system itself for effectiveness; and
- facilitating continual improvement

A company or organization that has been independently audited and certified to be in conformance with ISO 9001 may publicly state that it is "ISO 9001 certified" or "ISO 9001 registered". Certification to an ISO 9001 standard does not guarantee any quality of end products and services; rather, it certifies that formalized business processes are being applied.

Although the standards originated in manufacturing, they are now employed across several types of organizations. A "product", in ISO vocabulary, can mean a physical object, services, or software.

ISO 9000 series of standards

ISO 9001:2008 Quality management systems – Requirements is intended for use in any organization regardless of size, type or product (including service). It provides a number of requirements which an organization needs to fulfill to achieve customer satisfaction through consistent products and services which meet customer expectations. It includes a requirement for continual (i.e. planned) improvement of the Quality Management System, for which ISO 9004:2000 provides many hints.

ISO 9004:2000 Quality management systems - Guidelines for performance improvements covers continual improvement. This gives you advice on what you could do to enhance a mature system. This document very specifically states that it is not intended as a guide to implementation.

Summary of ISO 9001:2008

The quality policy is a formal statement from management, closely linked to the business and marketing plan and to customer needs. The quality policy is understood and followed at all levels and by all employees. Each employee needs measurable objectives to work towards.

Decisions about the quality system are made based on recorded data and the system is regularly audited and evaluated for conformance and effectiveness.

Records should show how and where raw materials and products were processed, to allow products and problems to be traced to the source.

You need to determine customer requirements and create systems for communicating with customers about product information, inquiries, contracts, orders, feedback and complaints.

When developing new products, you need to plan the stages of development, with appropriate testing at each stage. You need to test and document whether the product meets design requirements, regulatory requirements and user needs.

You need to regularly review performance through internal audits and meetings. Determine whether the quality system is working and what improvements can be made. Deal with past problems and potential problems. Keep records of these activities and the resulting decisions, and monitor their effectiveness (note: you need a documented procedure for internal audits).

You need documented procedures for dealing with actual and potential non-conformances (problems involving suppliers or customers, or internal problems). Make sure no one uses bad product, determine what to do with bad product, deal with the root cause of the problem and keep records to use as a tool to improve the system.

The ISO 9000 standard is continually being revised by standing technical committees and advisory groups, who receive feedback from those professionals who are implementing the standard.[28]

Certification

ISO does not itself certify organizations. Many countries have formed accreditation bodies to authorize certification bodies, which audit organizations applying for ISO 9001 compliance

---

[28] http://iso9001-consultant.co.uk/

certification. Although commonly referred to as ISO 9000:2000 certification, the actual standard to which an organization's quality management can be certified is ISO 9001:2000. Both the accreditation bodies and the certification bodies charge fees for their services. The various accreditation bodies have mutual agreements with each other to ensure that certificates issued by one of the Accredited Certification Bodies (CB) are accepted worldwide.

The applying organization is assessed based on an extensive sample of its sites, functions, products, services and processes; a list of problems ("action requests" or "non-compliances") is made known to the management. If there are no major problems on this list, or after it receives a satisfactory improvement plan from the management showing how any problems will be resolved, the certification body will issue an ISO 9001 certificate for each geographical site it has visited.

An ISO certificate is not a once-and-for-all award, but must be renewed at regular intervals recommended by the certification body, usually around three years. In contrast to the Capability Maturity Model there are no grades of competence within ISO 9001.

Auditing

Two types of auditing are required to become registered to the standard: auditing by an external certification body (external audit) and audits by internal staff trained for this process (internal audits). The aim is a continual process of review and assessment, to verify that the system is working as it's supposed to, find out where it can improve and to correct or prevent problems identified. It is considered healthier for internal auditors to audit outside their usual management line, so as to bring a degree of independence to their judgments.

Industry-specific interpretations

The ISO 9001 standard is generalized and abstract. Its parts must be carefully interpreted, to

> The TickIT guidelines are an interpretation of ISO 9000 produced by the UK Board of Trade to suit the processes of the information technology industry, especially software development.

make sense within a particular organization. Developing software is not like making cheese or offering counseling services; yet the ISO 9001 guidelines, because they are business management guidelines, can be applied to each of these. Diverse organizations—police departments (US), professional soccer teams (Mexico) and city councils (UK)—have successfully implemented ISO 9001:2000 systems.

Over time, various industry sectors have wanted to standardize their interpretations of the guidelines within their own marketplace. This is partly to ensure that their versions of ISO 9000 have their specific requirements, but also to try and ensure that more appropriately trained and experienced auditors are sent to assess them.

Advantages

It is widely acknowledged that proper quality management improves business, often having a positive effect on investment, market share, sales growth, sales margins, competitive advantage, and avoidance of litigation.[29]

According to the Providence Business News[30], implementing ISO often gives the following advantages:

- Create a more efficient, effective operation
- Increase customer satisfaction and retention
- Reduce audits
- Enhance marketing
- Improve employee motivation, awareness, and morale
- Promote international trade
- Increases profit
- Reduce waste and increases productivity

---

[29] "Probing the Limits: ISO 9001 Proves Ineffective". Scott Dalgleish. Quality Magazine April 1, 2005

[30] "Reasons Why Companies Should Have ISO Certification", Providence Business News, August 28, 2000.

Disadvantages

A common criticism of ISO 9001 is the amount of money, time and paperwork required for registration.[31] According to Barnes, "Opponents claim that it is only for documentation. Proponents believe that if a company has documented its quality systems, then most of the paperwork has already been completed."[32]

The standard is seen as especially prone to failure when a company is interested in certification before quality.[33] This is due partly because certifications (under these circumstances) are often based on customer contractual requirements rather than a desire to actually improve quality.

---

[31] "So many standards to follow, so little payoff". Stephanie Clifford. *Inc Magazine*, May 2005.

[32] "Good Business Sense Is the Key to Confronting ISO 9000" Frank Barnes in Review of Business, Spring 2000.

[33] "The 'quality' you can't feel", John Seddon, The Observer, Sunday November 19, 2000

CHAPTER 9
PRINCE2

PRojects IN Controlled Environments (PRINCE) is a project management method. It covers the management, control and organization of a project. "PRINCE2" refers to the second major version of this method and is a registered trademark of the Office of Government Commerce (OGC), an independent office of HM Treasury of the United Kingdom.

History

PRINCE2 is derived from the earlier PRINCE project management method, which was initially developed in 1989 by the Central Computer and Telecommunications Agency (CCTA) as a UK Government standard for information systems (IT) project management; however, it soon became regularly applied outside the purely IT environment.[34] PRINCE2 was released in 1996 as a generic project

---

[34] http://www.ogc.gov.uk/methods_prince_2__background.asp

management method.[35] PRINCE2 has become increasingly popular and is now a de facto standard for project management in the UK.[36] Its use has spread beyond the UK to more than 50 other countries.

The most current revision was released in 2009 as part of the Prince2:2009 refresh project[37] by the

PRINCE2:2009 Refresh: Since 2006, the method has been revised and launched as "PRINCE2:2009 Refresh" on June 16th. The name "PRINCE2" (instead of "PRINCE3" or similar) is kept to demonstrate that the method remains faithful to its principles. Nevertheless, it is a fundamental revision of the method from 1996 to adapt it to the changed business environment, to make the method simpler and "lighter", to address current weaknesses or misunderstandings, and to better integrate it with other OGC methods (ITIL, P3O, P3M3, MSP, M_o_R etc.). The main difference between the 2009 version and earlier versions is that there will be two manuals: 'Managing Projects Using PRINCE2' and 'Directing Projects Using PRINCE2'. Both the Foundation and Practitioner Examinations will be based on the new 'Managing Projects' manual and will not include material from the new 'Directing Projects' book. The pass mark for the Foundation exam will remain unchanged but the pass mark for the Practitioner exam will increase from the current 50% to 55% as of July 6th. The Practitioner exam will also shorten in length from 3 hours to 2.5 hours.

---

[35] http://www.ogc.gov.uk/news_2005_4333.asp
[36] http://www.prince-officialsite.com/
[37] *Managing successful projects with PRINCE2* (5th ed.). The Stationery Office. pp. 342.

Office of Government Commerce.

Description of the PRINCE2 method

Advantages

PRINCE2 is a structured approach to project management. It provides a method for managing projects within a clearly defined framework. PRINCE2 describes procedures to coordinate people and activities in a project, how to design and supervise the project, and what to do if the project has to be adjusted if it doesn't develop as planned. In the method each process is specified with its key inputs and outputs and with specific goals and activities to be carried out, which gives an automatic control of any deviations from the plan.

Divided into manageable stages, the method enables an efficient control of resources. On the basis of close monitoring the project can be carried out in a controlled and organized way. Being a structured method widely recognized and understood, PRINCE2 provides a common language for all participants in the project. The various management roles and responsibilities involved in a project are fully described and are adaptable to suit the complexity of the project and skills of the organization

Pitfalls

PRINCE2 is sometimes incorrectly considered inappropriate for very small projects, due to the work required in creating and maintaining documents, logs and lists. However, this may often be because of a misunderstanding about which parts of PRINCE2 to apply: PRINCE2 is fully scalable.[38]

---

[38] http://www.best-management-practice.com/Knowledge-Centre/Best-Practice-Guidance/PRINCE2/

CHAPTER 9: PRINCE2   107

Overview of the method

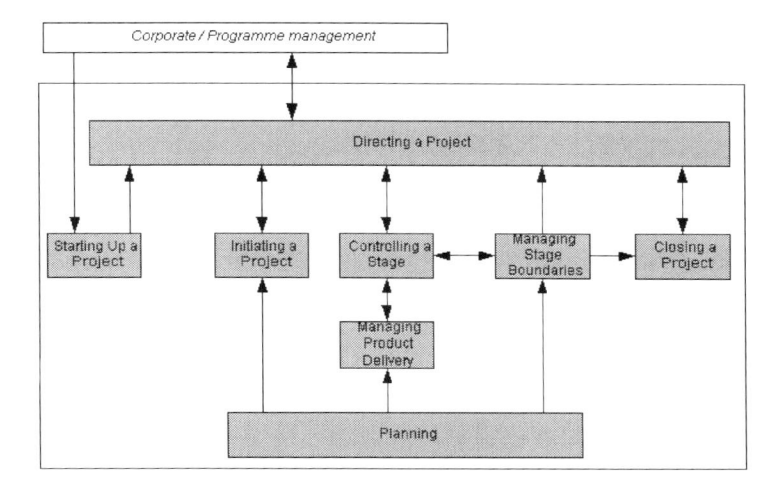

Diagram showing PRINCE2 processes.
The arrows represent flows of information.[39]

PRINCE2 is a process-driven project management method[40] that defines 45 separate sub-processes and organizes these into eight processes:

---

[39] http://en.wikipedia.org/wiki/File:Prince2_diagram.png
[40] http://www.ogc.gov.uk/methods_prince_2__whatisit.asp

Starting up a project

In this process the project team is appointed and a project brief (describing, in outline, what the project is attempting to achieve and the business justification for doing so) is prepared. In addition the overall approach to be taken is decided and the next stage of the project is planned. Once this work is done, the project board is asked to authorize the next stage, that of initiating the project.

Key activities include: appointing an executive and a project manager; designing and appointing a project management team; preparing a project brief; defining the project approach; and planning the next stage (initiation).

Planning

PRINCE2 advocates product based planning which means that the first task when planning is to identify and analyze products. Once the activities required to create these products are identified then it is possible to estimate the effort required for each and then schedule activities into a plan. There is always risk associated with any work and this must be analyzed.

Finally, this process suggests how the format of plans can be agreed and ensures that plans are completed to such a format.

Key activities include: designing a plan; defining and analyzing products; identifying activities and dependencies; estimating; scheduling; analyzing risks; and completing the plan.

Initiating a project

This process builds on the work of the startup process, and the project brief is augmented to form a Business case. The approach taken to ensure quality on the project is agreed together with the overall approach to controlling the project itself (project controls). Project files are also created as is an overall plan for the project. A plan for the next stage of the project is also created. The resultant information can be put before the project board for them to authorize the project itself.

Key activities include: planning quality; planning a project; refining the business case and risks; setting up project controls; setting up project files; and assembling a Project Initiation Document.

Directing a project

These sub-processes dictate how the Project Board (which comprises such roles as the executive sponsor or project sponsor) should control the overall project. As mentioned above, the project board can authorize an initiation stage and can also authorize a project. Directing a Project also dictates how the project board should authorize a stage plan, including any stage plan that replaces an existing stage plan due to slippage or other unforeseen circumstances. Also covered is the way in which the board can give ad hoc direction to a project and the way in which a project should be closed down.

Key activities include: authorizing initiation; authorizing a project; authorizing a stage or exception plan; giving ad-hoc direction; and confirming project closure.

Controlling a stage

PRINCE2 suggests that projects should be broken down into stages and these sub-processes dictate how each individual stage should be controlled. Most fundamentally this includes the way in which work packages are authorized and received. It also specifies the way in which progress should be monitored and how the highlights of the progress should be reported to the project board. A means for capturing and assessing project issues is suggested together with the way in which corrective action should be taken. It also lays down the method by which certain project issues should be escalated to the project board.

Key activities include: authorizing work package; assessing progress; capturing and examining project issues; reviewing stage status; reporting highlights; taking corrective action; escalating project issues; and receiving a completed work package.

Managing product delivery

This process consists of three sub-processes and these cover the way in which a work package should be accepted, executed and delivered.

Key activities include: accepting a work package; executing a work package; and delivering a work package.

Managing stage boundaries

The Controlling a Stage process dictates what should be done within a stage, Managing Stage Boundaries (SB) dictates what should be done towards the end of a stage. Most obviously, the next stage should be planned and the overall project plan, risk log and business case amended as necessary. The process also covers what should be done for a stage that has gone outside its tolerance levels. Finally, the process dictates how the end of the stage should be reported.

Key activities include: planning a stage; updating a project plan; updating a project business case; updating the risk log; reporting stage end; and producing an exception plan.

Closing a project

This covers the things that should be done at the end of a project. The project should be formally de-commissioned (and resources freed up for allocation to other activities), follow on actions should be identified and the project itself be formally evaluated.

Key activities include: decommissioning a project; identifying follow-on actions; and project evaluation review.

CHAPTER 10
ITIL

ITIL Overview

The **Information Technology Infrastructure Library (ITIL)** also known as Infrastructure Management Service (IMS) is a set of concepts and policies for managing information technology (IT) infrastructure, development and operations.

ITIL gives a detailed description of a number of important IT practices with comprehensive checklists, tasks and procedures that any IT organization can tailor to its needs. ITIL is published in a series of books, each of which covers an IT management topic. The names ITIL and IT Infrastructure Library are registered trademarks of the United Kingdom's Office of Government Commerce (OGC).

History

In the 1980s, the UK Government's Central Computer and Telecommunications Agency (CCTA) developed a set of recommendations, in response to the growing dependence on IT, and the recognition that without standard practices, government agencies and private sector contracts were independently creating their own IT management practices.

The IT Infrastructure Library originated as a collection of books each covering a specific practice within IT Service Management. ITIL was built around a process-model based view of controlling and managing operations often credited to W. Edwards Deming and his PDCA cycle.[41]

After the initial publication in 1989, the number of books quickly grew within ITIL v1 to over 30 volumes.

In 2000/2001, to make ITIL more accessible (and affordable), ITIL v2 consolidated the publications into 8 logical 'sets' that grouped related process guidelines to match different aspects of IT management, applications, and services. However, the main focus was known as the Service Management

---

[41] David Clifford, Jan van Bon (2008). *Implementing ISO/IEC 20000 Certification: The Roadmap*. ITSM Library. Van Haren Publishing. ISBN 908753082X.

sets (Service Support and Service Delivery) which were by far the most widely used, circulated, and understood of ITIL v2 publications.

In April 2001 the CCTA was merged into the Office of Government Commerce (OGC), an office of the UK Treasury.[42] In 2006, the ITIL v2 glossary was published.

In May 2007, this organization issued the version 3 of ITIL (also known as the ITIL Refresh Project) consisting of 26 processes and functions, now grouped under only 5 volumes, arranged around the concept of Service lifecycle structure.

In 2009, the OGC officially announced that ITIL v2 would be withdrawn and launched a major consultation as per how to proceed.[43]

---

[42] http://www.ogc.gov.uk/index.asp?id=1878
[43] http://www.ogc.gov.uk/guidance_itil.asp

Overview of the ITIL v3 library

Five key volumes comprise the ITIL v3, published in May 2007:

1. Service Strategy

2. Service Design

3. Service Transition

4. Service Operation

5. Continual Service Improvement

1. Service Strategy

As the center and origin point of the ITIL Service Lifecycle, the Service Strategy volume provides guidance on clarification and prioritization of service provider investments in services. More generally, Service Strategy focuses on helping IT organizations improve and develop over the long term. In both cases, Service Strategy relies largely upon a market-driven approach. Key topics covered include service value definition, business case development, service assets, market analysis, and service provider types. Processes covered include service portfolio management, demand management, and IT financial management.

2. Service Design

The ITIL Service Design volume provides good practice guidance on the design of IT services, processes, and other aspects of the service management effort. Significantly, design within ITIL is understood to encompass all elements relevant to technology service delivery, rather than focusing solely on design of the technology itself.

As such, Service Design addresses how a planned service solution interacts with the larger business and technical environments, service management systems required to support the service, processes which interacts with the service, technology, and architecture required to support the service, and the supply chain required to support the planned service.

Within ITIL, design work for an IT service is aggregated into a single Service Design Package (SDP). Service Design Packages, along with other information about services, are managed within the service catalog. Processes covered in this volume include service level management, availability management, capacity management, IT service continuity management, information security management, supplier management, and service catalog management.

3. Service Transition

Service transition relates to the delivery of services required by the business into live/operational use, and often encompasses the "project" side of IT rather than "BAU" (Business As Usual). This area also covers topics such as managing changes to the "BAU" environment. Topics include Service Asset and Configuration Management, Transition Planning and Support, Release and deployment management, Change Management, Knowledge Management, as well as the key roles of staff engaging in Service Transition.

4. Service Operation

Best practice for achieving the delivery of agreed levels of services both to end-users and the customers (where "customers" refer to those individuals who pay for the service and negotiate the SLAs). Service Operations is the part of the lifecycle where the services and value is actually directly delivered. Also the monitoring of problems and balance between service reliability and cost etc are considered.

Topics include:

- balancing conflicting goals (e.g. reliability vs. cost etc),
- event management,
- incident management,
- problem management,
- request fulfillment,
- access management, and
- service desk.

The functions include:

- technical management,
- application management,
- operations management,
- Service Desk, and
- responsibilities for staff engaging in Service Operation.

5. Continual Service Improvement (CSI)

CSI involves aligning and realigning IT services to changing business needs (because standstill implies decline).

The goal of CSI is to align and realign IT Services to changing business needs by identifying and implementing improvements to the IT services that support the Business Processes. The perspective of CSI on improvement is the business perspective of service quality, even though CSI aims to improve process effectiveness, efficiency and cost effectiveness of the IT processes through the whole lifecycle. To manage improvement, CSI should clearly define what should be controlled and measured.

CSI needs to be treated just like any other service practice. There needs to be upfront planning, training and awareness, ongoing scheduling, roles created, ownership assigned, and activities identified to be successful. CSI must be planned and scheduled as process with defined activities, inputs, outputs, roles and reporting.

Criticisms of ITIL

ITIL has been criticized on several fronts, including:

- The books are not affordable for non-commercial users
- Accusations that many ITIL advocates think ITIL is "a holistic, all-encompassing framework for IT governance";
- Accusations that proponents of ITIL in-doctrinate the methodology with 'religious zeal' at the expense of pragmatism.
- Implementation and credentialing requires specific training
- Debate over ITIL falling under BSM or ITSM frameworks

While ITIL addresses in depth the various aspects of Service Management, it does not address enterprise architecture in such depth. Many of the shortcomings in the implementation of ITIL do not necessarily come about because of flaws in the design or implementation of the Service Management aspects of the business, but rather the wider architectural framework in which the business is situated. Because of its primary focus on Service Management, ITIL has limited utility in managing poorly designed enterprise architectures, or how to feed back into the design of the enterprise architecture.

ITIL Alternatives

IT Service Management as a concept is related but not equivalent to ITIL which, in Version 2, contained a subsection specifically entitled IT Service Management (ITSM). (The five volumes of version 3 have no such demarcated subsection). The combination of the Service Support and Service Delivery volumes are generally equivalent to the scope of the ISO/IEC 20000 standard (previously BS 15000), "BS" meaning British Standard.

Outside of ITIL, other IT Service Management approaches and frameworks exist, including the Enterprise Computing Institute's library covering general issues of large scale IT management, including various Service Management subjects, and the Universal Service Management Body of Knowledge (USMBOK), developed offer a description of a service management system and service provider organization that may be universally applied to IT organizations and non-IT alike.

COBIT is perceived as an audit framework but the supporting body of knowledge (such as COBIT's books Control Practices, IT Assurance Guide, IT Governance Implementation Guide, and User's Guide for Service Managers) has grown to offer a credible alternative to ITIL.

The British Educational Communications and Technology Agency (BECTA) has developed the Framework for ICT Technical Support (FITS) and is based on ITIL, but it is slimmed down for UK primary and secondary schools (which often have very small IT departments). Similarly, *The Visible OPS Handbook: Implementing ITIL in 4 Practical and Auditable Steps* claims to be based on ITIL but to focus specifically on the biggest "bang for the buck" elements of ITIL.

Organizations that need to understand how ITIL processes link to a broader range of IT processes or need task level detail to guide their service management implementation can use the IBM Tivoli Unified Process (ITUP). Like MOF, ITUP is aligned with ITIL, but is presented as a complete, integrated process model.

Smaller organizations that cannot justify a full ITIL program and materials can gain insight into ITIL from a review of the Microsoft Operations Framework which is based on ITIL but defines a more limited implementation.

One United States - based approach to the enterprise lifecycle is found in *A Practical Guide to Federal Enterprise Architecture* by the U.S. CIO Council. This is a companion text to Federal Enterprise Architecture Framework (or FEAF). The guide ties together the operational (present time) CPIC (Capital Planning and Investment Control) processes, the architecture processes (future planning), and other pieces of the lifecycle management processes into one cohesive package.

CONFIGURATION MANAGEMENT

APPENDIX A
Acronyms

AA	Application Activity
ABL	Allocated Baseline
ACD	Allocated Configuration Documentation
ACO	Administrative Contracting Officer
AECMA	Association Europeenne des Construceurs de Materiel Aerospace
AFB	[U.S.] Air Force Base
AFM	[U.S.] Air Force Manual
AFR	[U.S.] Air Force Regulation
AGE	Aerospace Ground Equipment
AIA	Aeronautical Industry Association
AIS	Automated Information System
ALT	Alteration Instruction
AMSDL	Acquisition Management Systems and Data Requirements Control List
ANSI	American National Standards Institute
AR	[U.S.] Army Regulation

ARDEC	[U.S. Army] Armament Research, Development and Engineering Center
ASCII	American Standard Code for Information Interchange
ASTM	American Society for the Testing of Materials
BOM	Bill of Materials
CAGE	Commercial and Government Entity
CALS	Continuous Acquisition and Life-cycle Support
CCB	Configuration Control Board, Configuration Change Board
CDCA	Current Document Change Authority
CDR	Critical Design Review
CDRL	Contract Data Requirements List
CFR	Code of Federal Regulations
CI	Configuration Item
CITIS	Contractor Integrated Technical Information Service
CLIN	Contract Line Item Number
CM	Configuration Management
CMP	Configuration Management Plan

CNWDI	Critical Nuclear Weapons Design Information
CPIN	Computer Program Identification Number
CRYPTO	Cryptographic information
CSA	Configuration Status Accounting
CSCI	Computer Software Configuration Item
DCMC	[U.S.] Defense Contract Management Command
DDRS	[U.S.] Department of Defense Data Repository System
DED	Data Element Definition
DFARS	[U.S.] Defense Department Supplement to the Federal Acquisition Regulation
DID	Data Item Description
DIN	Deutsches Institute fur Normung
DLA	[U.S.] Defense Logistics Agency
DoD	[U.S.] Department of Defense
DODISS	[U.S.] Department of Defense Index of Specifications and Standards

DOE	[U.S.] Department of Energy
DOT	[U.S.] Department of Transportation
DTIC	[U.S.] Defense Technical Information Center
ECN	Engineering Change Notice
ECO	Engineering Change Order
ECP	Engineering Change Proposal
ECS	Embedded Computer Software
EDM	Enterprise Data Model
EEPROM	Electronically Erasable Programmable Read-only Memory
EIA	Electronic Industries Association
ELIN	Exhibit Line Item Number
Email	Electronic mail
FBL	Functional Baseline
FCA	Functional Configuration Audit
FCD	Functional Configuration Documentation
FFT	First Flight Test
FSC	[U.S.] Federal Supply Class

APPENDIX A: Acronyms

FSCM	[U.S.] Federal Supply Code for Manufacturers
GFD	Government-Furnished Documents
GFE	Government-Furnished Equipment
GFP	Government-Furnished Property
GLAA	Government Lead Application Activity
GPLR	Government Purpose License Rights
GPO	Government Printing Office
GSN	Government Serial Number
HEI	High Explosive Incendiary
HTML	Hypertext Mark-up Language
HWCI	Hardware Configuration Item
ICD	Interface Control Drawing, Interface Control Documentation
ICWG	Interface Control Working Group
IEEE	Institute of Electrical and Electronics Engineering
IFF	Identify Friend or Foe.
IGES	Initial Graphics Exchange Specification
IPT	Integrated Product Team
IRPOD	Individual Repair Part Ordering Data

ISO	International Standardization Organization
MACHALT	Machinery Alteration
MACHALTINST	Machinery Alteration Instruction
MICOM	[U.S. Army] Missile Command
MIL-STD	Military Standard
MIP	Modification Improvement Program
MRB	Material Review Board
MS	Military Standard
MSN	Manufacturer's Serial Number
MWO	Modification Work Order
NAS	[U.S.] National Aerospace Standard
NASA	[U.S.] National Aeronautics & Space Administration
NATO	North Atlantic Treaty Organization
NAVAIR	[U.S.] Naval Air Systems Command
NAVMATINST	[U.S.] Naval Materiel Systems Command Instruction
NAVSEA	[U.S.] Naval Sea Systems Command
NIIN	[U.S.] National Item Identification Number

APPENDIX A: Acronyms

NIST	[U.S.] National Institute of Standards and Technology
NOR	Notice of Revision
NSA	[U.S.] National Security Agency
NSCM	NATO Supply Code for Manufacturers
NSN	National Stock Number
NTIS	National Technical Information Service
NUCALTINST	Nuclear Alteration Instruction
NWS	[U.S.] Naval Weapons Station
OPEN	Object-oriented Process, Environment, and Notation (OPEN)
ORDALTINST	Ordnance Alteration Instruction
OSD	[U.S.] Office of the Secretary of Defense
OSHA	[U.S.] Occupational Safety & Health Agency
PAN	Procuring Activity Number
PBL	Product Baseline
PCA	Physical Configuration Audit
PCD	Product Configuration Documentation
PCO	Procurement Contracting Officer

PCTSS	Provisioning & Cataloging Technical Support System
PDM	Product Data Management [System]
PDF	Page Description File
PDR	Preliminary Design Review
PHST	Packaging, Handling, Storage, and Transportation
PIN	Part or Identification Number
POC	Point of Contact
PROM	Programmable Read-only Memory
RAC	Rapid Action Change [order]
RFD	Request For Deviation
SAE	Society of Automotive Engineers
SBIR	Small Business Innovative Research
SCN	Specification Change Notice
SDR	System Design Review
SFR	System Functional Review
SGML	Standard Generalized Markup Language
SHIPALT	Ship Alteration
SHIPALTINST	Ship Alteration Instruction

APPENDIX A: Acronyms

SIE	Special Inspection Equipment
SOW	Statement of Work
SRR	System Requirements Review
SSAN	Social Security Account Number
SSR	Software Specification Review
STANAG	Standard NATO Agreement
STEP	Standard for the Exchange of Product model data
TA	Tasking Activity
TCTO	Time-compliance Technical Order
TD	Technical Directive
TDP	Technical Data Package
TM	Technical Manual
TOPS	Technical Order Page Supplement
TPS	Test Program Set
U.S.	United States [of America]
USAF	United States Air Force
VDD	Version Description Document
VECP	Value Engineering Change Proposal
VHSIC	Very High Speed Integrated Circuit

WINTEL Warning: Intelligence methods and sources disclosed

APPENDIX B
Glossary

Definitions for configuration management terms used below are consistent with ANSI/EIA 649.[44]

Allocated Baseline (ABL). The approved allocated configuration documentation.

Allocated Configuration Documentation (ACD). The documentation describing a CI's functional, performance, interoperability, and interface requirements that are allocated from those of a system or higher level configuration item; interface requirements with interfacing configuration items; and the verifications required to confirm the achievement of those specified requirements.

Application Activity (AA). An activity that has selected an item or a document for use on programs under its control. However, it is not the current document change authority for the document(s).

Approval. The agreement that an item is complete and suitable for its intended use.

Approved Document (or Data). Document that has been approved by an appropriate authority and is the official (identified) version of the document until replaced by another approved version.

---

[44] MIL-HDBK-61A

Archived Document (or Data). Released or approved Document that is to be retained for historical purposes.

Assembly. A number of basic parts or subassemblies, or any combination thereof, joined together to perform a specific function. Typical examples are: electric generator, audio-frequency amplifier, power supply.

Computer database. See Database.

Computer software. See Software.

Computer Software Configuration Item (CSCI). A configuration item that is computer software.

Computer software documentation. Technical data or information, including computer listings, regardless of media, which document the requirements, design, or details of computer software; explain the capabilities and limitations of the software; or provide operating instructions for using or supporting computer software.

Configuration. The performance, functional, and physical attributes of an existing or planned product, or a combination of products.

Configuration audit. See: Functional Configuration Audit (FCA), and Physical Configuration Audit (PCA).

Configuration baseline (baseline).

(1) An agreed-to description of the attributes of a product, at a point in time, which serves as a basis for defining change.

(2) An approved and released document, or a set of documents, each of a specific revision; the purpose of which is to provide a defined basis for managing change.

(3) The currently approved and released configuration documentation.

(4) A released set of files comprising a software version and associated configuration documentation.

See: Allocated Baseline (ABL), Functional Baseline (FBL), and Product Baseline (PBL).

Configuration control.

(1) A systematic process that ensures that changes to released configuration documentation are properly identified, documented, evaluated for impact, approved by an appropriate level of authority, incorporated, and verified.

(2) The configuration management activity concerning: the systematic proposal, justification, evaluation, coordination, and disposition of proposed changes; and the implementation of all approved and released

changes into (a) the applicable configurations of a product, (b) associated product information, and (c) supporting and interfacing products and their associated product information.

Configuration Control Board (CCB). A board composed of technical and administrative representatives who recommend approval or disapproval of proposed engineering changes to, and proposed deviations from, a CI's current approved configuration documentation.

Configuration Control Board Directive (CCBD). The document that records the Engineering Change Proposal (ECP) approval (or disapproval) decision of the CCB and that provides the direction to the contracting activity either to incorporate the ECP into the contract for performing activity implementation or to communicate the disapproval to the performing activity.

Configuration documentation. Technical documentation, the primary purpose of which is to identify and define a product's performance, functional, and physical attributes (e.g., specifications, drawings). *See also: Allocated Configuration Documentation [ACD], Functional Configuration Documentation [FCD], and Product Configuration Documentation [PCD].*

Configuration identification.

(1) The systematic process of selecting the product attributes, organizing associated information about the attributes, and stating the attributes.

(2) Unique identifiers for a product and its configuration documents.

(3) The configuration management activity that encompasses the selection of CIs; the determination of the types of configuration documentation required for each CI; the issuance of numbers and other identifiers affixed to the CIs and to the technical documentation that defines the CI's configuration; the release of CIs and their associated configuration documentation; and the establishment of configuration baselines for CIs.

Configuration Item (CI). A Configuration Item is any hardware, software, or combination of both that satisfies an end use function and is designated for separate configuration management. Configuration items are typically referred to by an alphanumeric identifier which also serves as the unchanging base for the assignment of serial numbers to uniquely identify individual units of the CI.[45] *See also: Product-Tracking Base-Identifier.*

Configuration Management (CM). A management process for establishing and maintaining consistency of a product's performance, functional, and physical attributes with its requirements, design and operational information throughout its life.

Configuration Management Plan (CMP). The document defining how configuration management will be implemented (including policies and procedures) for a particular acquisition or program.

Configuration Status Accounting (CSA). The configuration management activity concerning capture and storage of, and access to, configuration information needed to manage products and product information effectively.

Contract. As used herein, denotes the document (for example, contract, memorandum of agreement/ understanding, purchase order) used to implement an agreement between a tasking activity (e.g., buyer) and a performing activity (e.g., seller).

Contractual acceptance of data. The action taken by the tasking activity signifying that an item submitted or

---

[45] Note: The terms "CI" and "Product" are identified as aliases in ANSI/EIA 649 and are used interchangeably within this handbook.

delivered by the performing activity complies with the requirements of the contract.

Current Document Change Authority (CDCA). The authority currently responsible for the content of a drawing, specification, or other document and which is the sole authority for approval of changes to that document. *See also: Application Activity [AA], Approval, Document Custodian Activity.*

Customer Repair (CR) Item. Any part or assembly which, upon failure or malfunction, is intended to be repaired or reworked by Government personnel (including contract personnel other than the original manufacturer.)

Data. Recorded information of any nature (including administrative, managerial, financial, and technical) regardless of medium or characteristics. *See also: Data item, Document.*

Database. A collection of related data stored in one or more computerized files in a manner that can be accessed by users or computer programs via a database management system.

Data item. A document or collection of documents that must be submitted by the performing activity to the procuring or tasking activity to fulfill a contract or tasking directive requirement for the delivery of information.

Defect. Any nonconformance of a characteristic with specified requirements.

Deficiencies. Deficiencies consist of two types:

    a. conditions or characteristics in any item which are not in accordance with the item's current approved configuration documentation; or

    b. inadequate (or erroneous) configuration documentation which has resulted, or may result, in units of the item that do not meet the requirements for the item.

Design change. *See Engineering change.*

Deviation. A specific written authorization to depart from a particular requirement(s) of an item's current approved configuration documentation for a specific number of units or a specified period of time, and to accept an item which is found to depart from specified requirements, but nevertheless is considered suitable for use "as is" or after repair by an approved method. (A deviation differs from an engineering change in that an approved engineering change requires corresponding revision of the item's current approved configuration documentation, whereas a deviation does not.)

Distribution Statement. A statement used in marking a technical document to denote the extent of its availability for distribution, release, and disclosure without need for additional approvals and authorizations from the controlling DoD office.

Document. A self-contained body of information or data that can be packaged for delivery on a single medium. Some examples of documents are: drawings, reports, standards, databases, application software, engineering designs, virtual part-models, etc.

Document custodian activity. The custodian of a document is the activity which is charged with the physical and electronic safekeeping and maintenance of the "original" document.

Document representation.

(1) A set of digital files which, when viewed or printed together, collectively represent the entire document. (For example: a set of raster files or a set of IGES files.) A document may have more than one document representation.

(2) A document in a non-digital form. (For example: paper, punched card set, or stable-base drawing.)

Engineering change.

(1) A change to the current approved configuration documentation of a configuration item.

(2) Any alteration to a product or its released configuration documentation. Effecting an engineering change may involve modification of the product, product information and associated interfacing products.

Engineering Change Directive (ECD). An internal performing activity document that indicates the approval of, and direction to incorporate or implement engineering change.

Engineering Change Proposal (ECP). The documentation by which a proposed engineering change is described, justified, and submitted to (a) the current document change authority for approval or disapproval of the design change in the documentation and (b) to the procuring activity for approval or disapproval of implementing the design change in units to be delivered or retrofit into assets already delivered.

Exchangeability of items. See *Interchangeable item, Replacement item, and Substitute item.*

Firmware. The combination of a hardware device and computer instructions or computer data that reside as read only software on the hardware device.

Fit. The ability of an item to physically interface or interconnect with or become an integral part of another item.

Form. The shape, size, dimensions, mass, weight, and other physical parameters that uniquely characterize an item. For software, form denotes the language and media.

Function. The action or actions that an item is designed to perform.

Functional Baseline (FBL). The approved functional configuration documentation.

Functional characteristics. Quantitative performance parameters and design constraints, including operational and logistic parameters and their respective tolerances. Functional characteristics include all performance parameters, such as range, speed, lethality, reliability, maintainability, and safety.

Functional Configuration Audit (FCA). The formal examination of functional characteristics of a configuration item, or system to verify that the item has achieved the requirements specified in its functional and/or allocated configuration documentation.

Functional Configuration Documentation (FCD). The documentation describing the system's functional, performance, interoperability, and interface requirements and the verifications required to demonstrate the achievement of those specified requirements.

Hardware. Products made of material and their components (mechanical, electrical, electronic, hydraulic, pneumatic). Computer software and technical documentation are excluded.

Hardware Configuration Item (HWCI). *See Configuration Item (CI).*

Interchangeable item. A product which possess such functional and physical attributes as to be equivalent in performance to another product of similar or identical purposes; and is capable of being exchanged for the other product without selection for fit or performance, and without alteration of the products themselves or of adjoining products, except for adjustment.

Interface. The performance, functional, and physical characteristics required to exist at a common boundary.

Interface control. The process of identifying, documenting, and controlling all performance, functional and physical attributes relevant to the interfacing of two or more products provided by one or more organizations.

Interface Control Documentation (ICD). Interface control drawing or other documentation that depicts physical, functional, performance, and test interfaces of related or co-functioning products.

Interface Control Working Group (ICWG). For programs that encompass a system, configuration item, or a computer software configuration item design cycle, an ICWG is established to control interface activity among the tasking activity, performing activities, or other agencies, including resolution of interface problems and documentation of interface agreements.

Interoperability. The ability to exchange information and operate effectively together. Item. A nonspecific term used to denote any product, including systems, materiel, parts, subassemblies, sets, accessories, etc.

Life cycle cost. The total cost to the tasking activity of acquisition and ownership of an item over its life cycle. As applicable, it includes the cost of development, acquisition, support, and, disposal.

Lot number. An identifying number consisting of alpha and numeric characters which, in conjunction with a manufacturer's identifying code and a Product-Tracking Base-Identifier, uniquely identifies a group of units of the same item which are manufactured or assembled by one producer under uniform conditions and which are expected to function in a uniform manner.

Manufacturer Repair (MR) Item. Any part or assembly for which user-maintenance is limited to replacement of consumables and that, upon failure or malfunction, is returned to the original manufacturer for repair.

Materiel. A generic term covering systems, equipment, stores, supplies, and spares, including related documentation, manuals, computer hardware, and software.

Modification Directive. The documentation that indicates the approval of, and direction to implement, a modification request.

Modification Request. The documentation by which a proposed modification of an asset is described, justified, and submitted to the asset owner (who is not the Current Document Change Authority for the asset design documentation) for approval or disapproval of implementing the modification in one or more units. A modification request may result in modification or installation drawings being created to describe the new configuration, but does not result in a revision of the existing design documentation for which an Engineering Change Proposal would be required.

Nomenclature.

(1) The combination of a Government-assigned designation and an approved item name. In certain cases, the designation root serves as the basis for assignment of serial and/or lot numbers.

(2) Names assigned to kinds and groups of products.

(3) Formal designations assigned to products by customer or supplier (such as model number, or model type, design differentiation, specific design series or configuration.)

Nonconformance. The failure of a unit or product to meet a specified requirement.

Nonrecurring costs. As applied an ECP, one-time costs that will be incurred if an engineering change is approved and which are independent of the quantity of items changed, such as cost of redesign or development testing.

Nonrepairable Item. Any part or assembly for which user-maintenance is limited to replenishment of consumables and replacement of the part or assembly upon failure or malfunction.

Notice of Revision (NOR). A document used to define revisions to configuration documentation which require revision after Engineering Change Proposal approval. *See also Engineering Change Proposal [ECP].*

Original. The current design activity's documents or digital document representation and associated source data file(s) of record.

Performing activity. Denotes an activity performing any of the requirements contained in a contract or tasking directive. A "Performing Activity" can be either a contractor or Government activity.

Physical characteristics (attributes). Quantitative and qualitative expressions of material features, such as composition, dimensions, finishes, form, fit, and their respective tolerances.

Physical Configuration Audit (PCA). The formal examination of the "as-built" configuration of a configuration item against its technical documentation to establish or verify the configuration item's product baseline.

Product Baseline (PBL). The approved product configuration documentation.

Product Configuration Documentation (PCD). A CI's detail design documentation including those verifications necessary for accepting product deliveries (first article and acceptance inspections.) Based on program production/procurement strategies, the design information contained in the PCD can be as simple as identifying a specific part number or as complex as full design disclosure.

Product-tracking base-identifier. An unchanging identifier used as a base for the assignment of serial numbers to uniquely identify individual units of an item or lot numbers to uniquely identify groups of units of an item. The product-tracking identifier is used rather than the Part or Identifying Number (PIN) because the PIN is altered to reflect a new configuration when the item it identifies is modified. The same product-tracking base-identifier may be used for several similar items (usually defined by a common document) and requires that each such item is assigned serial or lot numbers distinct from each other such item.

Product Tracking Identifier. A generic term that refers to the sequentially assigned alphanumeric identifier applied to a product to differentiate units of the product or groups of the product. This may be a

Government serial (or hull) number, manufacturer's serial number, lot number or date code.

Recurring costs. Costs that are incurred on a per-unit basis for each item changed or for each service or document ordered.

Release. The designation by the originating activity that a document representation or software version is approved by the appropriate authority and is subject to configuration change management procedures.

Released Document (Data):

(1) Document that has been released after review and internal approvals.

(2) Document that has been provided to others outside the originating group or team for use (as opposed to for comment).

Repair. A procedure which reduces, but does not completely eliminate, a nonconformance. Repair is distinguished from rework in that the characteristic after repair still does not completely conform to the applicable drawings, specifications, or contract requirements.

Repairable Item. Any part or assembly which, upon failure or malfunction, is intended to be repaired or reworked.

Replacement item. One which is interchangeable with another item, but which differs physically from the original item in that the installation of the replacement item requires operations such as drilling, reaming, cutting, filing, shimming, etc., in addition to the normal application and methods of attachment.

Retrofit. The incorporation of new design parts or software code, resulting from an approved engineering change, to a product's current approved product configuration documentation and into products already delivered to and accepted by customers.

Retrofit Instruction. The document that provides specific, step-by-step instructions about the installation of the replacement parts to be installed in delivered units to bring their configuration up to that approved by an ECP. (Sometimes referred to Alteration Instruction, Modification Work Order, Technical Directive, or Time Compliance Technical Order.)

Rework. A procedure applied to a product to eliminate a nonconformance to the drawings, specifications, or contract requirements that will completely eliminate the nonconformance and result in a characteristic that conforms completely.

Serial number. An identifying number consisting of alpha and numeric characters which is assigned sequentially in the order of manufacture or final test and which, in conjunction with a manufacturer's identifying CAGE code, uniquely identifies a single item within a group of similar items identified by a common product-tracking base-identifier.

Software. Computer programs and computer databases.

Specification. A document that explicitly states essential technical attributes/requirements for a product and procedures to determine that the product's performance meets its requirements/attributes.

Specification Change Notice (SCN). *See Engineering Change Proposal (ECP).*

Submitted Document (Data). Released document that has been made available to customers.

Substitute item. An item that possesses such functional and physical characteristics as to be capable of being exchanged for another item only under specified conditions or in particular applications and without alteration of the items themselves or of adjoining items.

Support equipment. Equipment and computer software required to maintain, test, or operate a product or facility in its intended environment.

Survivability. The capability of a system to avoid or withstand a hostile environment without suffering an abortive impairment of its ability to accomplish its designated mission.

System. A self-sufficient unit in its intended operational environment, which includes all equipment, related facilities, material, software, services, and personnel required for its operation and support.

Tasking activity. An organization that imposes the requirements contained in a contract or tasking directive on a performing activity, (for example, a Government Contracting Activity that awards a contract to a contractor, a Government Program Management Office that tasks another Government activity, or a contractor that tasks a subcontractor.)

Technical data. Technical data is recorded information (regardless of the form or method of recording) of a scientific or technical nature (including computer software documentation.)

Technical data package. A technical description of an item adequate for supporting an acquisition strategy, production, engineering, and logistics support. The description defines the required design configuration and procedures required to ensure adequacy of item performance. It consists of all applicable technical data such as drawings and associated lists, specifications, standards, performance requirements, quality assurance provisions, and packaging details.

Technical documentation. *See Technical data.*

Technical reviews. A series of system engineering activities by which the technical progress on a project is assessed relative to its technical or contractual requirements. The reviews are conducted at logical transition points in the development effort to identify and correct problems resulting from the work completed thus far before the problems can disrupt or delay the technical progress. The reviews provide a method for the performing activity and tasking activity to determine that the development of a configuration item and its documentation have a high probability of meeting contract requirements.

Training equipment. All types of maintenance and operator training hardware, devices, audio-visual training aids, and related software which: (a) are used to train maintenance and operator personnel by depicting, simulating, or portraying the operational or maintenance characteristics of an item or facility; (b) are kept consistent in design, construction, and configuration with such items in order to provide required training capability.

Version.

(1) One of several sequentially created configurations of a data product.

(2) A supplementary identifier used to distinguish a changed body or set of computer-based data (software) from the previous configuration with the same primary identifier. Version identifiers are usually associated with data (such as files, databases and software) used by, or maintained in, computers.

Waiver. *See Deviation.*

Working Document (Data). Document that has not been released; any document that is currently controlled solely by the originator including new versions of the document that were previously released, submitted, or approved.

ABOUT THE AUTHOR

Dr. Gary L. Vincent holds a Ph.D. and M.S. in Computer Information Systems and a B.S. in Business Administration Management and Psychology. He is certified in Levels I (Configuration Management), II (Software Configuration Management), and III (Enterprise Configuration Management) from the International Society of Configuration Management (ISSO). Dr. Vincent has worked on IT projects with the U.S. government for over 13 years, 5 of which in their CM Program.

Dr. Vincent is President of Vincent International Properties, Inc., and co-creator of the *Agelations* book and study courses on real estate investing, information marketing, and network marketing. He is also an international recording artist and business coach. He resides in West Virginia with his wife Carla.

QUICK ORDER FORM

Email Orders: Orders@BurningBulbPublishing.com

Fax Orders: 270-477-4512

Web Orders:
BurningBulbPublishing.com (click "Titles")

Postal Orders:
Burning Bulb Publishing,
P.O. Box 4721
Bridgeport, WV 26330-4721

Please send the following books (quantity/title):

_____

Name:_____

Address:_____

City:_____State:____Zip:_____

Telephone:_____

Email Address:_____

Shipping:
U.S.: $4.00 for first book and $2.00 for each additional product.

Printed in Great Britain
by Amazon